MW00879341

THEN I THOUGHT

of Home

Life Love Laughter

KELLY GRAY

xulon PRESS

Copyright © 2016 by Kelly Gray

Then I Thought of Home
Life Love Laughter
by Kelly Gray

Printed in the United States of America.

ISBN 9781498481762

All rights reserved solely by the author. The author guarantees all contents are original and do not infringe upon the legal rights of any other person or work. No part of this book may be reproduced in any form without the permission of the author. The views expressed in this book are not necessarily those of the publisher.

Scripture quotations taken from the King James Version (KJV) – *public domain*

Scripture quotations taken from the New International Version (NIV). Copyright © 1973, 1978, 1984, 2011 by Biblica, Inc.™. Used by permission. All rights reserved

To Contact Kelly Gray.

Email: kellyrayealltheway@gmail.com
Blog: www.thenithoughtofhome.blogspot.com or
Facebook: Then I Thought of Home-Kelly Gray

www.xulonpress.com

Table of Contents

REMOVE YOURSELF
FROM YOURSELF

I have several people tell me they love reading the blog and facebook posts.

I even have some tell me they want to come and live with us.

Others ask if things are really as good as they sound.

To which my answer is yes and no.

We do have a wonderful life. No doubt about that. I enjoy every bit of it.

It is also true we have days that are ugly. Days we lose our tempers. Say things that hurt.

Act selfish and lose our patience.

If you want to know the truth, there have been a couple of times when I've been glad we bought the other farm just so Mark would have someplace to go.

Come on now. Be honest, you know sometimes looking down the road at those tail-lights leaving is just what you need to be glad to see the headlights coming back.

I think your life, is a lot like my life.

That's why we connect. That's why you laugh or cry or feel something when you read the post.

When my family has those ugly moments, like me breaking the Christmas tree, or running over the lilac bush, or Mark says he is to busy to help me, or I come into the room to find the kids using the chain saw instead of a hand saw to trim the Christmas tree. Or whenever everyone complains about what we are having for supper, or I let us run out of towels, I find humor helps.

When you find yourself in those times, as we all do try this, remove yourself from yourself.

Pretend you are watching it happen in someone else's life and suddenly it is hysterical.

I mean really, most of the things that get us all upset are the very things we crack up at when we watch them on TV shows.

It is all in the way you look at it.

Like when I thought the channel locks had something to do with the TV, that made Mark mad.

But if I had not been his wife he would have thought it was funny.

That's why I am always telling him several times each day, "Honey, remove yourself from yourself. Pretend I'm someone else's wife and you will see how funny it is."

He is having a hard time catching on but it is working well for me.

Remember, the next time one of those heated moments comes upon you, remove yourself from yourself, pretend you are staring in a TV show, see the humor and let the stress slip away.

Let me know how it works for you!!

Treasures from Home

I have a fondness for stories of mothers long ago.

I enjoy reading of how Puritan mothers worked and cared for their families. How the Civil War mothers dealt with a divided country and maybe even a divided family. How she saw her home destroyed, crops lost and her sons killed, yet she got up and went on.

I think about the mothers that traveled out west in the wagon trains. I can only imagine the fear of sickness, or the possible loss of her children that was ever present as she journeyed on.

The mothers of the depression struggling to provide meals and keep clothes mended, the garden tended and a fire in the stove.

Or the World War Two mothers. I have had older women tell me they were afraid to go to the mailbox during that time, afraid of what they might find waiting for them there.

To be a mother is no small task. I'm afraid we have let it lose some of its importance. We don't honor it like we use to.

What about your mom? What do you remember her doing for you and the family? Did she sew, did she can, did she bake, did she encourage, did she correct, did she love your dad, did she care for aging parents or in-laws? Did she come home and make your favorite things, was she a room-mother? Was she a kind neighbor, did she expect manners in the home and expect to be treated with respect and respect, you in return?

The things we learn from mom are countless and price-less. The world couldn't function if it were not for so many of the things we learn at our mother's knees and from watching her hands.

We all have those things we have carried with us from our childhood homes into our homes today. Things learned from mom

I know I do.

What are the things you count as treasures from home?

Timeless Home Decor

It's not unusual for a woman to collect pictures or even keep a folder with decorating ideas for her house.

She may take them out and look at them, study them, plan how to make it happen. She probably even sits and dreams about the day when it's complete.

But how many of us have a picture of the "home" we want to build?

I heard this from a lady named Donna, she said we should draw a picture of our house and write inside the house the things we want our home to contain.

So I made a stick drawing of my house and inside I will write things like, joy, peace, comfort, stillness, encouragement, dignity, diligence, contentment on and on the list can go.

When I get my house filled in I'll hang it somewhere I'll see often. I'll be reminded I'm in a building process. So just like I would look for decorating ideas I'll start looking for ideas on how to encourage my family, or how to build a peaceful environment, how to impart joy to my family, etc.

It's important to decorate our homes, it's part of homemaking but what if we spent as much time on the real important things of home as we do the decorating of our homes.

One things for sure, the things we write in our stick house pictures will never go out of style. The structure of a real home is classic. It's timeless. The things that make it strong and beautiful will always be the same.

They stay constant from one generation to the next.

So get out your paper draw your house and start filling it in with the things you want it to be full of.

Then spend time filling it. You may have to look for ideas just like you do when you are decorating, that's okay, start a folder or a file of ways to emotionally build your home.

It's the one and only decorating project you will ever do that won't wind up going out of style.

15

That Home Feeling

There is just no way to tell you what home means to me. I guess that's why I named this book, Then I Thought of Home. I think God refers to Heaven as home because He knows how we all long for it.

When I was a girl I loved home. I always wanted company to come to my house more than I wanted to go to theirs.

Mom always made home, home. I always knew if I could just get home everything would be okay.

One of the sweetest things Mark ever said to me was about home. He was out working construction and got hurt. He told me when they were trying to help him he kept thinking, if I can just get home, Kelly will make it okay.

I loved hearing that. To know I had been able to carry the home feeling mom taught me about into my own home was a wonderful thing.

Today we've been working out in the weather, in the cold and the wind and the rain. I left for home before everyone else.

I left early to get that, "home feeling" prepared for them. You know what I mean. The light in the window, a fire in the stove and supper on the table.

The kind of things that feed your spirit and your body. The kind of things that give you courage and strength and excitement for the next day.

Home sweet home, there's no place like it and no place I would rather be.

How like our God to have Jesus go ahead and leave before us so He can be preparing that "home feeling" for us?

(John 14:2-3) My Father's house has many rooms; if that were not so, would I have told you that I am going there to prepare a place for you? And if I go and prepare a place for you, I will come back and take you to be with me that you also may be where I am.

I Want to Decorate My Life Like Grandma Did

Yesterday a friend and I were talking about decorating.

We talked about decorating country or old fashioned.

I started thinking about my Grandma's house, my grandma on my dad's side. I thought about my great aunts and the houses I grew up going into.

Most of them were country homes, farm houses.

I thought about how they were decorated.

I realized they really weren't decorated.

Do you remember a house like this somewhere?

One where the furniture lined the walls.

There was a fuel oil stove in the front room, that was the nice stove and a drum stove in the kitchen with a coffee can of soaking corncobs to start the fire with.

There was a calendar on the wall. An oilcloth on the table and a breadbox with a pie.

There were dishpans and dish drainers.

Three big meals a day were cooked and cleaned up and a bonnet was donned to go to the garden.

Clotheslines and chicken coops.

Canning time and butchering time.

A cellar lined with shelves and filled with home canned goods, lard was kept in five gallon buckets.

A telephone table with a rotary dial phone.

In the bedrooms there were featherbeds against the walls and a chest of drawers with an old round mirror up over it, not a bedroom suite just furniture serving the purpose. White lace curtains hung the window. There was another fuel oil stove in the back bedroom and the morning sun in the front bedroom.

There were no hallways you simply went from room to room.

There was a water bucket with a dipper on the back porch, and a cistern top was the side porch.

My grandpa would sit out there and smoke his cigar in the evening.

I guess when homes were used more they were decorated less, the less we use them for daily living the more we can decorate them.

I know women have always liked to make things pretty and our grandmothers did too. I guess they just understood where practical and pretty had to part ways.

So while the magazine pictures of old fashioned farm houses are beautiful and filled with old things I doubt very many of the true old fashioned farm houses looked that way.

As odd as it sounds, my grandmothers look, is the look I want.

I want the "life happens here" look.

While I don't want my furniture lined against the wall or a coffee can of corncobs by the drum stove, I do want a kitchen table that's used three times a day.

I want lace curtains and bread box with a pie

I want to sit on the porch at the close of the evening and reflect.

I want to have the wisdom to know when pretty and practical need to part ways and be okay with it.

I want to decorate my life like Grandma did.

Letters and Long Distance

When you turn on the road to Lost River Farm the first place you come to is an Amish farm.

Yesterday when the girls and I were coming down the road we saw Toby and his horses standing at the mailbox.

I knew exactly what he was doing, I could tell right away.

He was reading a letter.

I've heard them talk about getting letters from family.

He couldn't wait until he got to the house.

He stopped right there, opened it up and read it.

I was almost envious.

How long has it been since I got a good letter in the mailbox?

I can't even remember when.

I knew everyone back at his house would be excited to get the letter, they would either read it out loud or pass it around and maybe even both.

I bet they went back later and picked it up again and reread it.

They probably ran their hand over the paper.

It made me want to get a letter but maybe I should write one instead and make someone else happy.

I don't think we ever really get over going to the mailbox and wondering if there just might be a letter or card in there.

You know what else it made me think of?

Long distance phone calls.

Remember how rare and exciting they used to be.

I can remember coming in and everyone being around and listening to what the person on our end was saying.

I had two aunts that were long distance when I was growing up. I remember how mom laughed and laughed when she got to talk to them.

I also remember being careful about calling long distance.

It was a big deal and not to be taken lightly.

I guess letters and long distance phone calls remind me of when communication wasn't so easy or cheap.

I really am thankful for emails, and cell phones and all the things we have now but truth be told I don't think it is possible to replace the joy of a hand written letter from someone you love.

I think I'll buy some stationary and take up letter writing.

How about it? We can take something old and make it new again.

I'm going to write a letter this week and I hope you'll join me.

Think how fun it will be when someone has to stop right there at the mailbox because they can't wait to hear from you.

Happy letter writing everyone!!

Our Road Has Changed.

Our road has changed.

I don't mean the way it looks.

It's just the very same as it was the first time Mark and I drove down it twenty-five years ago this last April.

We were the young couple of the road.

The first place was a dairy farm. Our neighbors and their son and daughter-in-law ran it.

The first time I saw their son I described him to my mom as an older man. I laugh about that now, He was younger than I am now when I called him an older man.

Melvin would mow hay in the field across from our house and his little grandson would ride with him, (it had a cab) until he fell asleep and then Howard, Melvin's dad would come, Melvin would climb down out of the tractor with his sleeping grandson and hand him to his great grandpa who would take him back to the house.

I can still hear Olive calling the cows in and see her walking the fence row back to get them to be milked. Later on she got to where she would take the golf cart but she kept going.

She was still the main caregiver to her husband and mowing her own yard when she was 90.

If you continue down the road our place is next then on down and to the right is the Davis', Grace loved flowers and had so many different kinds. She had hummingbird feeders and would sit out in her chair in the evening and watch life. I remember her mowing also. We talked about the flowers and where she had got them and how to care for them.

Then on down to the left are the Haugers.. Lester and Ruby. Ruby passed away not long after we moved here and I didn't know her well. I do know Lester took very good care of her. We used to have Lester up for supper sometimes and he would tell us all about how things used to be around here. The road between our place and Lester's' floods out if we have a lot of rain and it stays closed for weeks. He told us about using a boat to get in and out when he was a boy and how the fence lines laid and all sorts of neat things.

On down the road and to the right is the Rippy's.

Franklin and Irene. Franklin died not long after we moved here. Irene was such a hard working woman. I can still see her quiet smile. As it turned out our oldest, Heidi, married Irene's grandson Paul.

Now Heidi and Paul live down a couple of roads over from our place.

Grace passed away yesterday.

Her husband Rex and Mark and I are the only ones left that were here twenty-five years ago.

Mark and I are the "older couple" now. It makes me see how fast life marches by.

It makes me sad..

I can go outside and see how it was.

I can see the cars and trucks they each one drove and see them waving as they passed by.

One of the good things is the farms all stayed within the families. There have been no sales and no auctions.

I love this road and I've loved the people that made it up.

They have all been the kind of people that you would want for neighbors. The kind of people who got up each day and did what needed to be done. They built a life one day at a time.

I'm so thankful and blessed to have known them all.

I think I understand now why people write songs about roads.

I know Mark's Uncle Glen preached a lot of funerals and my grandparents were a couple of them.

When they died we had the funeral at the church and then we had to pass by their house to get up to the cemetery. I remember Glen saying about Grandpa, "Well we've brought Theodore passed the homeplace for the last time."

That got to me.

I love homeplaces and the roads that take us to them.

Today when you leave your house and come to the end of your road and you have to stop, really stop.

Stop and look.

Take it all in.

One day it won't be the same because like our road, it will change.

Hide the memory of the road that leads to your home-place deep in your heart.

Believe me, later in life you will take it out, look at it in your mind's eye and treasure it.

I Adore the Sound of That

I'm sitting here listening to the sound of the wash machine. I adore that sound. Lots of times I hear it and think of my Grandma Marshall's wringer washer. I even go back longer ago and think about the wash tubs and scrub boards. I think about carrying water and heating water. I know years ago dirty clothes were dirtier than they are now. They were worn longer and washed less often.

Our clothes get really dirty. Not just dirt, but animal stuff, you know what I mean. Sometimes when I'm at Heidi's I glance in the laundry room. She has one little dirty clothes basket and the clothes aren't really even dirty. There's no dust, mud, animal stuff or stuff that can't be identified, it just a basket of nice clean dirty clothes. Then I come home to dirty chicken house clothes discarded in a pile in the garage, a running over basket in the downstairs bathroom and we won't even discuss the girl's dirty clothes basket, or is it a dirty clothes floor, or it could be a clean clothes floor, who is to know?

I think all of the above is enough to draw a picture of why I adore the sound of my washing machine. I don't want

Then I Thought of Home

to complain about my laundry. I mean really, what would my great grandmother think if she heard me complain? What would women in other countries think? What would the person loading their clothes up and heading to the laundromat think? Most importantly what would God think? He has given us so many clothes and when they get dirty, even really dirty, I sort them out, carry them to the back porch open the lid, pour in store bought detergent, add fabric softener, close lid, push button and wait.......now why wouldn't I adore the sound of that?

32

I've Been Found Out

What a day this has been. The appraiser was supposed to be here tomorrow so I was going to do big cleaning today. About nine this morning a man knocked at the door and I got a sinking feeling. I just knew it was him. I said, "Oh, I didn't think you were coming until tomorrow "he looked funny, glanced down at his paper and said, "You're right, I was supposed to be here tomorrow, sorry, do you care if I go ahead and do it today?" As any good Christian lady would do, I smiled, opened the door, lied, and said, "of course I don't mind, come on in." Everything down here was fine. Upstairs, not so fine. Jess uses her floor for a closet. I never go in Lucas' room. Heidi's old room has two air mattresses and a desk full of books in it and the girls' bathroom, well let's just don't even go there. I have been found out. He had to take pictures, I can only imagine what the picture of Jessica Joi's room looks like. When he got ready to leave he started to open the door, stopped, turned back to me and said, "Don't worry, her room can't hold a candle to my daughter's." I smiled and told him he was a nice man to say that. I wonder if he had to take a class in an appraisers' school about how to make embarrassed housewives feel okay. If he did, I'm sure he was at the top of his class.

Coming and Going

Mark just went out to check the birds again for the last time tonight. The house is quite and I'm left to think back over the day.

That's one of my favorite things to do before bed, sort of skim my memory journal. I like to enjoy the high points all over again.

I like to do a mental re-do of my day. I like to think about the coming morning. I love, love, love morning. I think I always have. I like to think about getting up and making the coffee. If dawn had a scent it would be coffee. It was made for mornings. I think about what I'm going to make for breakfast and how happy my family will be when it's served. I wonder if there will be a deer in the field and if there will be a morning mist. I think about the work I will get done before everyone gets up and I think about curling up in my chair and reading my Bible. I think about the prayers my family and friends will need tomorrow.

I look forward to the crisp, freshness of a new morning keeping in mind before I get to my new morning I've got to have tonight. I love clean sheets and warm blankets in a cold room. I like it so cold my nose turns red. At night I get in my bed and I shiver. Not because I'm cold but because I'm so happy. I'm so thankful. I never go to bed that I don't thank God for my bed. I'm so humbled that my family is safe. There are no guns or bombs. I have a home and it's a safe place. I don't know about tomorrow night but for tonight, me and mine are safe, fed and sheltered and that's all I ever need.

I guess that's why I always take time to skim the day over, it reminds me I have just had the perfect day, both coming and going.

Wrapped in a Sunset

One of my favorite things is a sunset. Our bedroom window faces west and the evening sun comes in and it casts a certain light over the room, it's like a signal to me, almost like the sun is tapping on the window, calling me outside to watch the show.

Something about the moments before a sunset brings a sense of urgency. I remember digging sweet potatoes in the fall, the evening was cool and the ground was cold. I was watching the sky and knew the sun would soon be setting. We dug as quickly as we could, trying to get finished before the darkness came. I've been packing tomatoes on the back of the truck when the sky started to cast those brilliant colors, it's like it was warning me time was almost up. I remember watching the sunset with the kids as we walked toward the house. It's a good feeling to watch the day end and know you've been a part of it. To know you've got the work that belonged to that day done and you can start tomorrow with a clean slate. When darkness falls the sense of, "hurry," leaves. It is what it is, and you've done what you could do... There's no need to hurry now. You slow down and walk toward the house. You notice the light in the window and the smoke curling out of the chimney, and you think about the perfectness of the day.

Who but God would think to wrap up the gift of a day in a sunset?

A Day Like No Other

Sunday is one of my favorite things. It's a day like no other. Every day of the week is a gift but I think of Sunday as being the big gift sitting on the table with all the other days around it and you have to open the little ones before you get the big one.

I like to think of all that will be going on today. I like to think of all the houses where moms, or grandmas are getting up early to prepare Sunday dinner. None of the kids even know how much work they put into it but they know they look forward to it every week.

Maybe they have a game of some sort or shopping, or the simple Sunday afternoon drive or a nap on the couch. Every one celebrates Sunday in a different way.

God is good like that. He gives us what he knows our bodies and souls are crying for after a week of toil. He gives us a day of rest and reflection. A day of choices. A day to remember Him or a day to go on like usual. He told us what He wants for this day and then He sets us free to do with it what we chose.

Sunday is the Lords Day, God's gift to us. It really is a day like no other. I want to remember Him in all I do.

Here's wishing you a happy day like no other day!

Learning to Work

This morning when I left I met two little Amish boys in a buggy coming toward home.

Mark said they had been out delivering berries.

They oldest one was probably ten and the one standing up in the back of the buggy was younger.

They waved so happily.

I couldn't help but think how they were out and being productive.

They were out of school and they were working.

They were learning responsibility and what it means to be a part of the team.

If they don't do their job and do it well it hurts the family.

At a young age they learn to feel important and of value.

They learn about money, how you make it and how you save it and what it really means.

They know how much work dollars translate into.

If someone gives them eight dollars for a gallon of straw-berries and they look down at it in their hand, it means more to them than to someone who never spent the morning in a berry patch.

They learn work is money and money is work and that's an important lesson that is being lost in today's time.

I shared a post the other day about the lessons learned on a farm.

The blessings of being a farm kid.

Farm kids take on responsibility early.

When Heidi and Lucas were seven and five they had the total responsibility of feeding and bedding 14 bottle calves.

They went out morning and night and mixed the milk, cleaned and filled the bottles feed the calves, cleaned the stalls and bedded them.

When Jess and Liv came along they followed suit.

I guess I'm saying all of this because when I passed those boys today it made me think about how blessed my family and our neighbors are to live like we live and where we live.

God is good.

The Heart of Hospitality

We all know if you look up the word hospitable in the dictionary it comes between the words, hospice and hospital.

That just seems right doesn't it?

Both the words hospice and hospital are about comfort. They're about meeting the needs of someone else and making them comfortable or better.

Isn't that what we're doing when we're hospitable?

What comes to mind when you think of someone being hospitable, or better yet who comes to your mind? Who makes you feel that way?

Hospitality is more about a person's heart than the place.

It's also about what's needed at the time.

Sometimes showing hospitality means bringing out the best dishes, and cloth napkins. It means place cards, candles and flowers.

I love those times. Times when you make everyone feel like they are someplace fancy because they are someone fancy.

Other times it might be beans and cornbread served in the everyday dishes.

Or it may even be a fresh brewed cup of coffee with a friend or a stranger after you've pushed all the papers and things on the table to the other end.

It might be filling a dinner plate, rolling a fork in a napkin and filling a quart jar with sweet tea for your husband to take to the man who is hauling for you but can't stop to come to the house so he eats on the run.

When Mark and I lived in Lubbock for a while we went to church one Sunday night and an older couple, (probably same age we are now) invited us over. We had never met them before. We went home with them and she fixed us hot tea and fruitcake. I was feeling homesick and she was hospitable. I have loved fruit cake ever since.

One time Mark's Uncle Glen told about how he would go to town and see someone he hadn't seen for a while and so he would ask them over for supper.

He would go home and tell Aunt Pat and she would get busy getting things ready, He said she would clean and cook and make him clean and cook.

He said by the time the company got there he had worked so hard he wished they weren't coming. I love that story because we can all relate.

We worry and stew about having things just right. I do the very same thing.

Sometimes people hesitate to open their homes because they think they aren't nice enough or clean enough or big enough.

When my kids were small my house was in a constant state of disarray.

I always told people, if you want a drink, I'll wash you a glass and if you want to sit down I'll move the toy. Just know you're always welcome.

Well, I moved on from that now and while I don't have to move anymore toys you could on occasion catch me needing to wash a glass.

It's also important to remember opening our house does not mean showing our house.

The house should just be a back drop to the feeling.

When we have someone over it's about them not how we have decorated, or how clean or messy our house is, what we have or don't have.

A lot of the pressure of hospitality would fall away if we could only remember that.

The other happy thing about hospitality is you don't even have to be home to be hospitable.

We can make people feel welcome and comfortable at work, at school, church in the parking lot or store.

It's really all about how we receive others.

I heard a story about a lady who went to a dinner party and was seated between two very important state officials.

She said when she talked to the first one she was very impressed by how important he was and all he had done.

After she talked to the second man, she felt very important and pleased with herself.

You see the first man had talked about himself, the second man had asked about her.

It really can be that simple.

Just take time to care.

You can't care for everyone, and no one is expecting you too, but we can all care for someone.

So pick someone, pick someone every day to be hospitable to.

Remember it's about the other person and your spirit of hospitality, not the house.

Make your heart hospitable and hospitality will flow from it

Enjoy the Journey

Jessica and I went to Seymour yesterday.

I've always loved that drive; I know it's a little long but it's so pretty.

Really the drive into or out of Salem is pretty from every direction.

My favorite part of the Seymour drive is when you cross over into Jackson county from Washington county.

Remember how you come down the Millport Knob and are surrounded by trees as you drive through? It's beautiful then all of a sudden you are down the knob, you cross the Muskatatuck River and the view changes drastically.

The trees and knobs are gone and it's wide open fields. Just vast amounts of openness.

I imagine that's how the explores felt when they would come to a clearing or prairie land after cutting their way through forest.

I got to thinking that's just how life is too.

We go along not being able to see what's around us or right in front of us. We can't imagine what's ahead and then suddenly we come into a clearing.

We see the things we couldn't see before, there was to much stuff in our way.

Sometimes life is like coming down out of the knobs and suddenly all the stuff is gone and you can see clearly.

Other times the stuff may still be there, like when you cross the Muskatatuck, you can still see a few trees but you're able to see around them and get a focus on other things.

I love those times when you see clearly, when you have focus and purpose.

But truth be known I enjoy a good walk through the woods too.

I guess the key is to enjoy the journey no matter where you find yourself because it is sure to change at any given moment.

Respecting The Property of Others

You know how I am and how I get to thinking about things.

That seems to be a family curse or blessing, we think a lot.

We take things apart and wonder about them.

So here I was thinking, well actually remembering which quickly turned into thinking.

Thinking about having respect for what belongs to others.

I remembered once when my brothers and I were young we went to Grandpa and Grandma's with dad.

Grandpa gave us some cucumbers and when it was time to leave us kids and the cucumbers all got in the back of the pick-up, you know back when we did stuff like that.

Anyway we hadn't got very far from Grandpa's, we hadn't even made it to Martinsburg yet, if you know the area we were on 335 right before the curve by the quarry.

Sorry, back to the story, we got an idea to throw one of those cucumbers at the speed limit sign, so we did.

Bad idea....

My dad stopped that truck on a dime got out of it and was standing at the side of the bed in lighting speed.

I know someone was spanked or we were all spanked and I mean days of old type spanking not today's spankings. But I don't so much remember that.

What I do remember is how bothered my dad's face looked.

It had upset him we had been so disrespectful.

He asked us if we owned that sign or the cucumber.

Of course we didn't.

He told us that sign was government property and was to be treated with respect.

The cucumber was grown by our grandparents and given to him and we had no right to use it to throw at something.

I will never forget that lesson.

We were never allowed to open food and eat it while going through the store. I never let my kids do this either.

That seems a small thing but it is a good way to teach them about respect. You see until that food is paid for, they don't own it and it needs to be treated like it's the property of someone else.

We were taught not to be touching other people's cars in the parking lot or anywhere.

I did the same with my kids. I can remember one day getting Jessica out of the car seat and Heidi and Lucas were standing beside me and they were touching the car beside us.

I did what my parents did with us, I just explained how that car did not belong to us so we shouldn't be touching it.

They weren't hurting it but it was just the idea of it. Just part of learning to respect the things of others.

These are just a couple of small things but they went a long way in teaching both me and my children the importance of respecting what belongs to others, be it the government, a store or someone you don't even know.

It falls under the category of doing unto others as you would have them do unto you or your things.

It's part of honoring others above yourself.

It's part of a bunch of over-arching values.

Which brings me back to my subject, teaching respect.

How are you teaching your children respect and value of the property of others?

How do you show it yourself?

It can be as simple at putting your cart up at Wal-Mart. You know little things like that do matter.

It matters to you when you are trying to park and carts are where they aren't supposed to be, or when one hits your car, and it matters to the kid who gets sent out to bring the carts in and his job is longer and harder just because someone else didn't show respect.

You know it makes you feel good to treat people and their things right. You getting a feeling of making the world a better place.

That's the feeling you want your children to catch, not that you're getting after them for everything but they are becoming a respectful person and enjoy being a part of the big picture and making things right as much as we can in our own little corners of the world, even if it's just a grocery store parking lot. It all matters.

So back to the question, how are you acting this out in your life and the life of your family.

Five Things I Don't Like About The Farm

Remember my post about the things I love about the farm?

Well, recently I've been reminded about the things I don't love about the farm.

1. Flies. Now I have a high fly tolerance, I'm used to them but I never cease to be amazed when I go to someone's house for a cookout and we can actually eat outside. That could never happen here. We can sit outside fine, but eating is a whole different story. Flies are the uninvited guest to every attempted picnic.

2 Rough Yards. Our yard used to be a cow pasture. Now we're not the type to lay sod or hire landscape people or anything like that. So our yard is rough. Well, I thought it was rough until I mowed at Lost River yesterday, now that's rough. I think it was a cornfield before it was a yard, which is even worse than a pasture. It left me thinking what it would be like to have a sod yard or better yet a lawn service.

3. A garden that is acres instead of plots or raised. We don't garden like we used to but our garden used to be right at two acres. I always look at those raised beds and think how fun they look. Little raised beds seem fun. Two acres of field...not so much.

4. Manure. I don't like manure on clothes or on the floor on in the truck, but what I like makes no difference because it continues to frequent those places.

5. Livestock on the loose, but that's another story.

As I'm sitting here looking over my list of dislikes I'm glad it isn't as long as my likes.

If the end of the day, or in this case the beginning of the day, finds you having more of life to like than dislike, I think that a happy thing.

So I guess I'll take the flies, the rough yards and the used to be huge garden since it comes with beautiful sunrises and sunsets, new pigs, calves, chicks and kittens. Planting and harvest. Excitement and stillness.

"Waitin on a Farmer"

I've often thought someone should write a song like Brad Paisley's "Waiting on a Woman." Something from the woman's point of view, maybe even a farm wife's point of view.

You know what I mean, there could be a line about waiting in a truck in a field.

Or waiting at the parts place.

Or waiting for him to call and tell you which field to come to or which part to get.

There might even be a line about waiting by the window at night and looking for headlights when he is much longer than he said he would be.

One thing is for sure, there would have to be one about waiting for him to come in and get cleaned up when he knows full well you are supposed to be somewhere in a short time and he is doing that one more thing he always thinks he has time to do before he can quit for the day.

I'm thinking there should be a part about when he asks you to come and go with him to the other farm because he has a quick repair to make. You know better but he looks that cute way he looks and so you go. It's good and daylight when you leave and when darkness falls you are still sitting in the truck waiting for him to finish the repairs or worse yet, you are out there with him in the dark holding the flashlight and every time you start to let the light droop he in no uncertain terms lets you know you are not keeping the light steady. You put the light back where it should be and then you study him. You are looking for that cuteness you thought you saw earlier, you know, that cuteness that got you in the middle of a field in the dark holding a flashlight.

This list could go on and on.

If you are a farm wife you are probably making one as you read.

Yep, it's got to be done, someone has got to write a song about a farm wife waiting on her farmer.

So who is it going to be?

This evening while you're waiting on that farmer man you love and it's for sure we love them, jot down what you think the perfect country and western song line would be about a farm wife waiting on her man.

I can't wait to read your thoughts.

Who knows we could all be called up on stage at the next Country Music Awards show.

Now wouldn't that be something?

Some of My Favorite Things About the Farm

In honor of National Ag Day, I thought I would simply blog about the simple things I love about the farm.

1. Finding new kittens in the barn.

2. The contented sound a sow makes as she lets her milk down to feed her babies.

4. The way the barn smells when the cows are feeding.

5. Dogs in the back of a pick-up truck

6. The smell of hay and the view from the loft.

7. Watching a couple of men stand in the middle of a field talking then bending down to get a handful of soil, standing back up and letting it slowly sift through their hands back to the ground.

8. When you top a hill along the road just as the crops are popping up and the rows are so green and straight and distinct.

9. The smell of the dirt in the air.

10. Giving dirty little kids who have played outside pushing trucks and tractors in that bare spot in the yard a bath at night and finding a little shiny nose underneath all those smudges.

11. Combines and semi's in the fields at harvest time.

12. The way the leaves of the corn sound like ocean waves when the wind blows.

I could go on and on but I'm going to stop because I want to know your favorite things.

Please feel free to add to the list, I can't wait to read your thoughts and then say, "Oh yeah, I love that too!"

What Would I Do Without That Man

When Mark and I were young and the children were small people would often tell me I should have a career because if something happened to Mark I wouldn't know what to do.

I know that was said in love but I still could never figure it out. Why would I spend my life doing what I may never have to do and miss out on what was my job to do at the time?

I always knew if something happened I would do whatever needed to be done. I didn't worry about it and to be honest I didn't think about it much either.

So what's happened to me?

Why do I worry now?

The older we get the more I appreciate him and ask myself, "what would I do?"

Not so much what would I do financially but what would I do without him being here by my side?

The more I watch him pulling on his coveralls, coat and gloves as he goes out in the still dark of the morning or I watch the truck headlights coming up the chicken house road at night or see him working on one of the girl's cars or talking to Lucas on the phone or getting up to go kiss Heidi goodbye before she goes back home I feel scared.

I feel my heart squeeze and I think, what would I do without him?

How could we ever go on without him?

How could I ever know what he knows and do what he does and be what he is?

Does it take being with someone for almost thirty-one years to become so one with them you don't know where they end and you begin?

It seems like if I was ever going to question how I would hold on it would have been when I was young with four little ones, not now when they are grown.

Yet here I am, feeling what I guess so many women before me have felt.

Things that a woman feels when she has loved, lived, worked, farmed, struggled and overcame with the husband of her youth.

I guess it's no wonder I watch him, no wonder I treasure him and feel afraid of a life without him.

We're a part of each other. We're one.

I guess that's the way it's meant to be.

I'm so glad when we were young I made being his wife and mother of his children my career of choice.

It's been my best move ever and the older we get the more I realize it.

I hope this will be an encouragement to you if you are young and life is hard right now.

I hope it encourages you to hang on because that man you married will grow sweeter to you every day.

Then one day you'll look out the window at him coming in the driveway and you'll be so glad to see him one more time and you'll ask yourself, "What would I do without that man?"

So You Want to Date a Farmer

So you want to date a farmer?

It isn't for the faint of heart or the insecure.

You'll need to be sure of who you are, what you can do and what you want.

For instance, you can't take it personal and get all upset when they don't show up to get you until nine or ten o'clock at night.

I mean after all; you know you can't stop working while the sun is still up.

Don't worry, you will learn to enjoy waving at all your friends as they are going home from their dates and you're just leaving. Secretly they'll be jealous and wishing their night was just beginning too.

Be prepared to sit in a farrowing house for hours while he helps deliver pigs. At first you'll think they're cute and he is sweet for caring so much but that will pass. When it does you just act like it didn't and keep on sitting there.

You may find yourself in a hot hayfield while they load wagons.

Learn to like to sit on hay bales. You will be doing a lot of it.

All of these things will become dear to you. You'll discover that you are not faint hearted, that you do know who you are, and what you want, and what you want is him and his way of life.

You will find you love sitting on a bale of hay waiting for him to finish milking. You'll feel proud when you learn to know his farm and barn like he does. You will know how much the hog weighed that they fattened out in that certain pen and what kind of personality the cows have. Which field produces the best and where water stands when it rains.

You will love getting wild flowers he finds in the field for you. One of the things you'll find yourself doing while you're looking out the window for his headlights to appear so you can go out is daydreaming of what it was like when he got you the flower. You'll imagine him seeing the flower, thinking of you, stopping the tractor and getting off to pick it and bring to you.

You will thrill in those times when you come to an electric fence going to the barn and he picks you up and puts you over.... you better thrill because things will change and he won't be doing that anymore or if he does it won't be as easy.

You'll enjoy watching him throw hay and duck your head and smile when you see him looking back to see if you're watching him.

Then one cold night when you least expect it you'll be sitting there in that freezing barn while he is over there milking and he will ask you to marry him.

He is kneeling down but it's because he is milking not because he is proposing.

But you won't care,

It's so perfect and so right, it's so him.

Of course you will accept and another farm will be started.

You will buy a piece of land and begin to write your own story.

Things will be hard for a while, he won't have much free time and he will have even less money. But you will keep working, days will turn into weeks and weeks, into months and months into years and one day you will be in a place you could have only dreamed of, you won't know how you got there for sure because all you did was get up every day and together you did the work that was before you to do.

You will have built a farm and raised a family.

Then one day your son will bring a girl home and you will watch out the window as she goes with him to the barn, or the hayfield or wherever there is work to be done.

You will turn from the window and while you put up the plate you've been drying you'll give thanks that all those years ago you decided to date a farmer.

Then like all mothers you will jump into the future and start thinking about where you will have your husband build the new swing set you will no doubt be needing for your grandbabies when your son marries that young lady he's walking through the yard with and the circle begins to spin all over again.

New Romance VS. Old Romance

I have always liked to have supper ready for Mark when he comes in.

Even when we didn't have children and I worked outside the home I always enjoyed coming home and seeing to it that he had a good supper.

I would want to set the table pretty and serve it just so.I wanted him to look at it and think, "wow!"

Well, I now know he didn't really care about the table setting but he liked the meal.

If it's cold out I think about what they would like to eat when they come in. If it's hot I think about what would be cool and refreshing.

As you know it was a cold day yesterday, Mark came in and while he was getting cleaned up I felt this surge of excitement about getting his plate ready for him. I was so glad I could do that.

But then..........He came out of the bathroom and headed for his chair.

Another surge shot through me. Only this one was a negative one. This surge said said to me, "hey, he is expecting you to fix his plate, he is expecting you to bring it to him." Then the surge suggested I be out-raged. I mean of all the nerve, just expecting me to bring his plate to him.

So, I was.

Out-raged I mean.

But only for a moment.

Isn't that how selfishness works?

I had looked forward all day to serving Mark. Truth is I should serve Mark. Truth is it is okay for Mark to expect me to serve him, to love him.

Marriage works best when you are able to expect things from your spouse.

Think about it, what kind of marriage would it be if you couldn't expect good things from your husband or wife?

It doesn't mean Mark is taking me for granted because he was expecting me to fix his plate.

It means he has learned after almost 30 years that I like to do that. (I'll let you in on a little family secret, one of the things he does when he is mad at me is fix his own plate, I think he thinks that will really get to me.... It does.)

I said all that to say this, I like it that he knows I am going to take care of him. I like it that I know he is going to take care of me.

I like knowing that when we have a flat tire he is going to get out and fix it while I sit in the car and I like knowing he knows he can go sit down and I'll bring him his plate.

There is a lot to be said for the excitement of a new romance, but I'm finding there can never be enough said for the comfort, trust and excitement of an old one.

Honey, There's a Snake in the Bed

I've never been much of a dreamer.

I mean as far as having dreams while you sleep.

Mark on the other hand is a huge dreamer and an active dreamer.

Like just now. I got up and went into the kitchen and had just lifted my fork to take a bite of cake when I heard him get up and start walking toward the kitchen.

Of course I quickly put down my fork and acted like I was getting a drink of water, however there was no need.

He was completely out of it, he had no idea I was about to eat cake or that I was pretending to drink water.

He was talking to me about the new blanket I bought for the bed and how nice it was.

I never bought a new blanket. Awake and in his right mind Mark Gray would never notice anything like a new blanket no matter how nice it was.

I took a bite of cake and mumbled I was glad he liked the blanket, he told me good night and went back to bed.

Once when we were building the chicken barns I woke up to find him sitting at the end of the bed with my foot in his lap.

He had a hold of my big toe and was twisting it.

I asked him what he was doing, and he said, he was working on a water line and had to get this piece off and started twisting my toe again.

I screamed and kicked him until he let go.

One other time I woke up to find him looking under the bed, I asked him what he was doing, he said he was looking for the baby. I asked him what baby, he said, you know the kind you keep under the bed.

The worst one was the time he told me there was a snake in the bed.

You see once we did have a snake get in the house we were renting at the time.So I thought it could true.

So there we were lying there face to face and he says to me "Honey, there's a snake in the bed"

I knew he could be dreaming so I said to him, 'Do you realize what you are saying?"

He said, "Yes, there is a snake in the bed"

So I laid there and thought to myself, what does one do when there is a snake in their bed, do you jump real fast, do you lay real still, what should I do.

About that time Mark said something completely crazy and I knew he was dreaming and there was no snake in the bed.

Well, except the one I turned into because I was so upset.

I think I kicked and screamed that time too.

Some of the Things I'll Never Get Right

No matter how hard I try, there are things I will never get right.

Here's a small list.

I will never turn the ignition right when Mark is working on the car and wants me to try and start it.

I will never pump the brakes right when he is trying to bleed them.

I will never apply the gas correctly or turn correctly when Mark is trying to get me out of the ditch.

(yes, I do get in the ditch. One time I ran off the road in the snow and had to walk home. When I got home and told Mark he asked me if the car was hurt? I told him I didn't think so, but I couldn't tell for sure because there was to many trees on top of it. He just turned and walked down the road toward the car in silence. I followed.)

I will never bring the right tool when he calls for one. (just a hint to all you ladies, channel locks don't have anything to do with the TV, so don't look there.) Your husband will mutter many things under his breath if he finds out that's where you are looking.

I will never get it right when any type of livestock gets out. If I move when its charging at me, he will say, I should have stood my ground and not let it by.

If I stand my ground and let the said livestock run over me, it will be said I should have had enough sense to get out of the way when it was coming through.

The only solace I have is all the things Mark will never get right.

I won't list them though, his sense of humor isn't as good as mine and it might not go over well.

Don't Be Afraid of the Challenge or the Challenger, They Can Be Your Friends

We all need someone in our lives who expects us to be more than we are at the current time.

Most of us don't like that kind of person, but we need them just the same.

We like being around people who make us feel okay the way we are, we say things like, "They accept me just as I am."

That's normal and there is truth in that thought, the problem is to our hurt we abuse the thought.

We like it so much we twist truth to make it apply.

Take the song, "Just As I Am" for example, or Jesus and the woman taken in adultery, now there is a misused piece of scripture.

We all come just as we are, we can come no other way but the problem is in our pride we think we can come just as we are and stay that way.

There is never an example of a single person in the Bible who came to Jesus, and I mean really came to Jesus and stayed the same.

That just can't happen.

We always say Jesus didn't condemn the women taken in adultery and that's true, He didn't, but He also didn't leave her where she was or how she came.

He told her to go and sin no more. He was telling her go and be more, go and be new, don't walk this way anymore.

We tend to want to take that story and make it mean where she was at in life was okay, read it again you will find that's not what it's saying at all.

Don't be afraid when someone asks you for more, when someone challenges you to be a better at work, at home at church, wherever you find yourself, don't be afraid when you're asked to step it up.

If you have someone in your life who is challenging you don't just assume they're being over the top to quick.

Try to learn, try to grow, try to give more. Don't just blindly accept good as good enough

(let me throw in a disclaimer here, I know we all know of weird controlling situations I'm not talking about that,)

I'm talking about not being afraid to examine ourselves and see if we really are giving less than what we can give or being less than what we can be.

We've got to be real about who we are and where we are before we can move on to who we want to be and where we want to go.

After the examination we'll find we are strong in areas and we'll find we're weak in others. Then we can concentrate on our strengths and minimize or weakness's.

It's okay to not be okay, none of us are. What's not okay is to never move forward, to never grow to never reach.

Be content with who you are and where you are but never think that's all there is.

Be ready to accept the challenge.

Go ahead examine yourself, be glad for where you are strong and ready to work where you are weak.

Remember having a challenge or a challenger in our life can work to our good.

Living Life in Due Season

If you've been with me on this blog adventure for very long at all you know I talk a lot about the seasons of life.

The older I get the more I see how important it is we know our season and more importantly accept our season and live it to the fullest.

All throughout history there has been a marking of the seasons in people's lives.

When you were a child, you were a child.

One of the biggest jobs of a child was to play. They played at being adults.

They dreamed of being the grown up.

Little boys put on dad's hat and spent the day pretending to do what men do.

Little girls did the same, together they played house, and family.

The acted out what grown-ups did.

Have you noticed you don't see children pretend to be grown- ups as much as you used to?

Have you noticed how often grown- ups keep pretending to be young?

When did growing up become a thing to fear or get around or put off?

When did our seasons become so blurred?

There is a time for everything but not all at the same time.

When you are a newlywed you can't expect to have what the couple who has been married for forty years has.

That's okay. They didn't have it in the early season either. They lived day by day and the seasons changed and next thing you know, they had.

When we're young parents, we're young parents. We can't live like we're still in the no children or the grown children stage.

There are things we won't be able to do or if we do them we will do them at a great cost. The cost of losing time as a young parent that can never be replaced. When things happen continually in the wrong season it wreaks havoc not only in nature but in the seasons of our lives as well.

Don't be afraid of your season. Don't think you have to have it all right now.

There are many things I thought I would like to do and even had the opportunity to do.

But I knew it wasn't my season. I was in the season of young motherhood. No matter what people say my life was not my own.

I had children to raise.

My time would come.

We have to be willing to wait for the season to change if we don't nothing will be right, but if we flow with the passing of time and take each season in its place the beauty is unreal.

I guess I say all of that to say this.

Don't cram to much into your life or you won't enjoy any of it. Don't blur your seasons by lingering to long in one or by jumping into the next one.

I know I use this word a lot but it's one of the keys to a happy life, SAVOR, SAVOR, SAVOR.

Accept your season, do the things that are to be done in that season when they are to be done and you'll find yourself free to enjoy the next one.

Oh I know there are things we can't control; things often don't turn out like we thought but truth be told there is a lot we can control. So do what you can about how you are living now so you can live better later.

Everything in due season.

It's how it's meant to be and how it works best.

So slow down and live the season you're in and remember while you can't have all of the fruits of life at once you can have all of the ones that are in season at the time. That's the only way to insure you won't miss anything.

No matter what society tells you, living life in due season is the only way you will ever look back and really see you have had it all.

Life is like fruit, it's always sweetest when it's picked in season.

Be the Momma. It Matters

I've heard it said that Moses' mother gave her time and her life to Moses' and his siblings and therefore God gave the world Moses and his siblings.

Wow, being a momma mattered.

Just think by giving our time and our lives to our children we're giving great things to the world!!

It could be as simple as waking them with gentleness or making a cup of hot chocolate.

You might decide to let something go today so you can listen to them.

It might be a little gift or a compliment.

It might mean you need to say that hard thing you've been putting off. You might need to be a little more consistent.

Or it could be a back rub or their favorite meal.

How will you purposely plan to give your time and life to being a Momma today?

Remember, it matters.... and remember even when it doesn't feel like it, when you're, "The Momma" you're everything in your family's world.

To Many Irons in the Fire

I read this and thought it was good.

She is only identified as Cindy and this is what she said.

"I see my first priority as being a wife and homemaker. Even though I have to work, that is a secondary calling. I want to make my home a place of rest, peace, and order. I want it to be a haven where God's character is reflected through my actions and speech as well as my creative gifting."

I liked this because we tend to get caught up in the working away mom or the working at home mom debate.

This lady says she has to work out of the home but she sees her home as first priority.

What does that mean?

One thing it can mean is while she has to work she is careful not to get to many other irons in the fire.

This is true for stay at home moms too.

I've seen many a stay at home mom have so many outside obligations such as clubs and boards and groups that they were seldom home.

Even homemakers' meetings can be one iron to many if they keep you too busy to home make.

As usual Satan is always pushing us to go a little more away from home all the time.

Stop, slow down and pay attention to what you are doing, working mom and stay at home mom alike.

If you are gone to work all day, then try not to be gone all night.

If you are home all day the same is true, don't be gone all evening.

When your kids are young or even teens for that matter, be willing to put a lot of activities on the back burner.

Now isn't the time to be on several boards or community task forces or even to many church programs.

All of those things are good but if we all keep leaving our home places without mom in the day and evening it won't matter how many community activities we have because the community will become a mess.

Someone has to mind the fort and it might as well be us.

When you really think about it who else would you want to mind your fort but you?

Probably no one.

While my kids were home I was about the business of being at home.

I didn't belong to a lot of groups and I didn't go out a lot.

Being a wife and mother was stress enough so I didn't want to be taking on other stress.

I didn't want my mind to be three different places when I only had the emotional and brain power to be in one at a time.

I had to make a lot of choices about what I was going to do and how I was going to live.

I don't say all of this to say I did it right.

My mistakes as a mother show up more all the time now that my kids are grown.

I have stayed awake at night crying over my mistakes many times.

If you've been a mother for as long as me mistakes will be a thing you have to learn to live with.

So what am I saying, I'm saying we still have to take precautions, we still have to be careful, I'm saying don't get to many irons in the fire.

While you are in the children at home season, be they little or teens, be at home.

Other things can wait, the home and family won't.

If you have to many things going on take an honest look at them, start deciding which ones can go.

Get a little pile of foam hearts and houses and when you make your schedule out put a home or heart out on the table for each activity you have chosen to take part in.

When you've finished you will have a good picture of where you are giving most of your heart too and where you spend enough time to call home.

Sometimes we don't realize how much time we are gone from our family, sometimes we have to see it laid out on the table in front of us.

Maybe you don't really need to be on that board.

Maybe going back to school can wait for a little bit.

Maybe you really can replace your night at the gym with family walks after supper.

The list goes on and on.

We think busy makes us good, we like to be able to tell people how busy and crazy and packed our lives are.

Why?

Why do we do that?

How much sweeter to not live that way.

Just live a fulfilled, quiet, happy life and people will see, your family will be blessed and you won't need to say a word.

Every kitchen should have a cast "iron" skillet and not just because they fry beautiful chicken or make golden cornbread but because they can remind us it's hard to keep a good eye on to many skillets.

Moral of the story, let's try not to get to may irons in the fire.

What Made Me Who I Am

I was in a conversation recently about what makes you who you are.

I guess we all wonder that at times.

I thought about myself and what made me like I am.

I know we live in a time when everyone wants to blame their upbringing for the way they are.

It is true none of us get raised without some type of emotional scars.

Our parents, no matter how much they loved us didn't do it all right, there were times they were busy and insensitive.

Times they were short with us and we may have been spanked when we didn't deserve it.

We vow to do better and in many ways we do but still we fail.

Our children will have hurts and insecurities they will be able to trace back to us.

Thankfully that's not the end of the story though.

Thankfully most of us had parents that did a lot of things right too.

We were fed and we were clothed.

We had a bed to sleep in at night.

We were sent to school and educated.

I was thinking about my childhood.

My dad worked hours and hours, he worked away all day at a public job and every night at my Grandpa's farm and his own farm.

We were Mom's career. She was a homemaker.

We didn't have a lot but I never felt poor, it was a shock to me when I learned others thought we were.

I remember having a friend home with me one day and she said, "You're poor aren't you?"

I felt uncomfortable and confused, I told her I didn't know.

Isn't that wonderful?

I didn't know.

Why didn't I know?

I didn't know because of the way I was being raised.

I was never made to feel poor and I never went without.

Our lunches and school books were always paid for in cash by my parents.

If something was going on at school and a new outfit was needed, we had one.

If we wanted to play an instrument one was rented.

I don't know how they did it, I know it was all they could do, but they did it.

I'm so proud of my parents, I'm so thankful for who they taught me to be.

Years went on and things got easier for mom and dad, then I married and I was poor again.

Mark and I didn't have much I once again found myself surprised and uncomfortable when I realized others saw us as poor.

I didn't feel poor.

We were paying for our place, buying our groceries and paying our bills all though it often took us a while to get them paid.

I never felt anything but blessed.

Do you remember in the Bible when the Apostle Paul said, I have learned to be content?

He said I have been in want and I have had plenty.

I feel like that is my story.

I think that is part of what made me who I am.

I have been what people considered poor but we kept at it and worked together every day until finally we had.

I'm not saying we have lots but we have what we need.

I'm so thankful for all of it and the attitude of contentment I saw lived out before me.

I'm thankful for all the people and the experiences that have made me who I am and I'm glad God has been gracious to me and allowed me to open my eyes and realize all of it.

Be a Blessing and Those Closest to You Will Reap a Sweet Harvest

When you sow seeds of kindness you will reap a sweet harvest.

Or as in my case someone close to you may receive a blessing as a result of your kindness.

If you have ever been in Sunday school with me, you have heard this story but if not I want to share it to encourage you to always go the extra mile. Your family will be blessed if you do.

When I was a girl I remember my mom packing an extra lunch sack when we went on field trips at school.

She would tell me to take it because there might be some little boy or girl who forgot to bring something.

There always was someone.

I can remember my teacher coming and asking me if I had an extra lunch.

She had taught my brother so she knew my mother.

I told her yes.

I wasn't as kind as my mother and even though I said yes deep in my heart I wanted those extra Frito's for myself because we didn't get them often. Nonetheless, I gave it to her.

This all happened when I was in lower elementary so now let's fast forward and I'm a junior in high school.

I left school at noon daily to go to a job training school.

My best friend Julie went with me or I with her.

One day we stopped at Long John Silver's to get lunch.

I ordered and went to pay and couldn't find my money. I had lost my lunch money.

I told the lady waiting on me I was sorry but had lost my money and wouldn't be able to get my meal.

I went over to sit down with Julie and almost instantly there was a lady beside our table with my food.

She said, "Honey, I couldn't help but overhear what happened to you. I have four girls of my own and I would hope if they were ever out and this happened to them someone would take care of them so I bought your lunch."

I was so got. I didn't' know what to say. I tried to tell her no but she wouldn't hear of it. I asked for her address so I could send the money and she wouldn't do that either. There was nothing to do but accept her kindness and thank her.

After she left my mother flew to my mind.

I thought about all those children she had made sure had a lunch years ago.

Now here I was, years later, her daughter, the one without a lunch and in God's kindness to my mother He had sent another mother to care for me.

I was only 17 then but I was old enough to see that I had been blessed because my mother blessed.

Be a blessing to someone today because you never know when those who mean the most to you will reap a harvest from it.

Gator Ride

We went for a gator ride before supper.

We hadn't even got a quarter of a mile down the road before I knew I should of brought the camera.

There were two deer in Melvin's field.

Big pretty deer they had a reddish tint to them.

We went on down to PD Baker road and saw another deer then when we got to Possum Hollow we saw two more than three more on Posey chapel. That's not counting the wild ducks and geese and a fox too.

Hay is down everywhere and the fence rows are hanging full of honeysuckle and blooming Tiger Lillie's.

The air could not have been sweeter.

I noticed every little thing I could so when I go to bed tonight I can see it all again.

Have a good night everyone.

Sleep well.

Summer Storm

Mark said he needed me to come and run the loader over at Lost River today.

When I left it was so hot and humid and the sky looked dark to the west.

The leaves were turning over on the trees like they do when it gets windy before a storm.

When I got almost to Drew Road I could see the wind picking up the dust on the road and blowing it across the field.

I love to see the snow blowing across the field in the winter and I love to see the wind picking up the dust and carrying it away before a storm on a hot summer day.

And then I really love the rain that rides in on the wind because it washes away all that dust on my car. :)

Twang, Dialect or Accent
I Like Them All

When I first started my page I would post a word a week that we don't use much anymore.

Words I didn't want to see pass from our vocabulary.

I used words like quaint, yonder, davenport, pocketbook, commence, pert near of course you say it as one word, or that's the way my grandpa said it, pert near, meaning almost or pretty near.

I like words.

I like dialect and accents.

Everyone says we have a southern accent.

Lots of times people think Mark is from Texas when they hear him talk. His voice is deep and he sounds like the south.

Lucas and the girls talk real slow and drag their words out and you can tell they are from the country.

Heidi and I talk real fast and use our hands and our eyes get big. Sometimes we twang but we're quick about it when we do. :)

I heard on the news that dialects are becoming a thing of the past.

Television and radio have gone a long way toward making us all speak the same.

Dialect is "untaught" in schools.

I understand they think it makes you sound smarter if you don't twang or drag out your vowels like we do in the south and the country or add an r sound to words like they do in the northeast.

Just because I understand what they are thinking doesn't mean I agree though. As I said earlier I enjoy a good accent or dialect.

To be honest I hope we don't lose either one.

I hope we will always be able to hear the sound of the part of this country someone was born and raised in.

It's something to be proud of. It's who your people are and how they talk. It's their language, it's our language.

I have more words listed that I don't want to forget to use from time to time. I want to keep them alive.

I hope you do too. I hope you will think about words that you like words you haven't heard in a "spell" and jot them down. Teach them to your children or grandchildren.

Oh they may not care so much now but a word spoken is a word heard and a word heard is a word learned.

One day they'll remember, they'll add it in with all their new words of the day.

The new is good but speak the old too.

So go ahead and have a blast from the past.

What word will you use in conversation with your family this week that might have them saying, "What?"

Woman Be Healed

She was tired of living this way, she had tried everything men had to offer, none of it worked.

When she came to the end of herself and the end of earthly possibilities she reached out to Jesus.

She reached out and touched him and she was no longer the same.

She was made new.

If you are at the end of all earthly possibilities, reach out for him and be made new and if you aren't at the end of them, act like you are, by- pass them, don't even try that way anymore.

Luke 8: 46 But Jesus said, "Someone touched me, I know that power has gone out from me."

You will never come to Jesus and not be noticed, he will notice. You won't get lost in the crowd, he won't miss you... he will see you and feel you and you will be loved, and protected.

Me and My Prayer Problems

Does prayer come easy for you?

I have a lot of conversational type prayer. You know what I mean don't you?

The kind of prayer or conversation you have on and off all day long with God.

You don't actually stop and begin a formal prayer but you are talking with Him and sharing your day.

Then there is the end of the day prayer.

That's a tougher one.

How many times have you fell asleep while praying?

If you are like me more than you would like to tell about.

Then there is the last minute, I better hurry up and pray type of prayer. I've had my share of those as well.

Today I'm talking about planned prayer time.

Is it hard for you to pray during planned prayer time.

Does your mind go blank or does it wander away?

Do you even find yourself bored sometimes?

Do you sometimes feel like there is nothing to pray about even though the world is spinning out of control all around us?

I can answer yes to all of those questions, I've felt all those things.

A prayer journal seems to help me with a lot of those prayer problems.

I have a couple of pretty ones and I have some that are just bound notebooks. I have some that are just scrape pieces of paper I scrawled on when it was pray or lose my mind and I didn't have my journal.

I don't know why but there is something about writing your prayers.

Give it a try if you never have, even if you think you are not a writer. When you write it is easier to stay focused.

When you start to write a prayer of thanks or supplication for a family member you will be reminded of another family member and then you will start writing about them.

When you write about what's going on with one friend your other friend will be brought to your mind and you will start praying for them too.

Sometimes when I'm whining to God the best way for me to catch myself is to see it in print. Then I look at it and think, "oh no, you didn't see that did you God?" Written prayer can be a real good form of self-evaluation.

When I look back at my prayer journal I can tell my state of mind by my writing. If I'm upset as in mad upset, I write real big and fast and sloppy. I guess it's a shouting prayer or that's how it looks anyway. My spirit is shouting. I notice that after a bit it returns to normal size.

I guess I had found the peace I had come looking for.

Sometimes I like to look back over them and see the things that have been answered, other times I look back over them and think, have I really been praying about this for that long?

Sometimes I go back and read my prayers and think, boy, did you really write that, this is good. I say to myself, maybe I better put this one toward the front then when I die someone will see it. They may even read it at my funeral and say, "Boy could she pray."

Other times I read what I prayed about and think I better tear this out and burn it lest I die and someone find it. I would never want anyone to know I thought this or did that.

Sometimes when I'm looking back I'm blessed to see where I am compared to where I was.

Sometimes I've been going forward and sometimes my prayer journal has shown me I was slipping.

The written word doesn't lie.

You will find things out about yourself that maybe you couldn't see until they had been written.

I don't keep every prayer I write, that would be unwise.

Sometimes things are better thrown away but the act of writing your prayer can be a release and you'll find there is no need to keep it.

I hope you will take some time to write your prayers.

You will be amazed at how much more focused you will be.

Oh you may still sit there and stare at the paper for a few minutes but once you put pen to paper your heart will take over and your hand will start moving and either you or the things you are praying about will start changing.

It might happen fast or you might pray for years but you can rest assured in a world where it feels like no one is listening and it's hard to be heard, God is listening, He hears you.

I always like to imagine God sitting up in His throne, leaning forward with His ear bent toward earth when I pray.

I like to think He doesn't want to miss a word.

Don't wait another day, stop by the store or raid your kids school supplies and start your prayer journal today.

You will never be sorry, and remember God is sitting up and leaning forward just waiting for you to begin. He doesn't want to miss a thing you have to say.

Berry Picking

The Amish are picking our berries at Lost River.

Heidi, Ez and I were over there and then Mark pulled in he had the trailer because he was going to get the tractor and bring it back home.

There were three Amish children there picking.

The oldest, a girl, was about 12 or 13 and the other two were boys and they were younger. They had come over in a little cart and had the cutest little pony pulling it.

Heidi and I went on down toward the chicken houses while Mark stopped to talk to the kids.

The youngest boy, Mark said he was 8 came over to the truck and stood there with his leg bent a little and his hand in his pocket he already had the stance of a man as he stood there and talked to Mark.

I smiled and Heidi did too.

Mark came on down the lane and stopped I handed him Ez through the window so he could pretend to drive down to the barns.

Ezra loves that, he was really farming. :)

Mark called the cows and while we were all standing there watching them eat he told us Amos, the little boy, told him they were getting along good.

They were getting a lot.

Mark said Amos had a berry stain from one side of his face to the other.

So Mark told him he would get along even faster if he would stop eating so many of them.

Amos laughed and Mark laughed and Amos ate another berry.

Springtime, little boys and berry stains that's a sweet part of life. <3

Butchering Time

The snow today got me to thinking about butchering time.

You could only butcher when you were going to have several cold days in a row and often it was snowing.

When I was a girl we did all our own butchering.

My grandpa, dad and uncles butchered for themselves and others.

I could never stand to watch them shoot the hogs or cows, I stayed away until that was done.

I remember them skinning the cows and hanging them in the barn for a few days to cool out.

I can still see those big ole steers and hogs pulled high up in the barn.

If I remember right the beef was always butchered at Grandpa's but I think the hogs were slaughtered in different places because I remember Grandpa bringing the scolding box to our house.

They built a fire under the scolding box and when the water was hot enough they dipped the hog in a few times then rolled him over on a prepared surface and scrapped the hair off.

I remember the first time I ever helped do that. That was probably the only time.

My grandma's kitchen stands out in my mind to this day. I see my aunts all making sausage.

The men would grind it on the back porch and carry it in the kitchen where there would be several big dish tubs and the spices would be added and the mixing would begin.

When the other meat was sliced there would be someone to tear the paper off, someone to put the right amount of meat per package, depending on whose family we were doing at the time, someone wrapped and someone wrote on the package. There was always a job for everyone.

We learned to eat liver, heart, brains, tongue and all.

My kids all like tongue better than I do.

We made lard and of course that meant we had cracklings.

Lard was put in five gallon buckets. One of us kids was always sent to dip the lard when Grandma or mom needed some.

We always had plenty of meat.

When we were young if we were having friends over we got to pick the meal. We always picked lunch meat.

A lunch meat sandwich was a treat to behold.

My kids have all said the same thing. They would get so tired of eating steak. We ate steak all the time and didn't even know what we had.

We had no idea the cost of it because we always had it.

It's a good feeling to carry all those boxes of meat in and fill your freezers. There was a feeling of well-being when your freezer is full and your shelves are stocked.

To be able to feed your family is one of the greatest blessings ever. It's our most basic need and to have it fulfilled is huge.

You never look at any kind of harvest be it crops or a full freezer or a thriving garden and stocked shelves without a great sense of gratitude and humility.

When you live close to the land you never forget "All come from dust, and to dust all return." Ecc. 3:20

The circle completes itself and it's an amazing thing.

Sometimes God Just Plain and Simple Calls Me On It

Sometimes I don't listen well.

Sometimes I don't want to do what I know I should.

Several years ago Mark hurt my feelings.

He didn't even know what he had done, he soooo didn't know what he had said, and that hurt even more. Had he said it in anger or something I could have excused it but he was perfectly fine it was just an honest statement.

I didn't say anything but I went into the bedroom, locked the door and pulled the covers up over my face and cried and asked why I had ever married him. You know sort of like a grown mature Christian woman would do. (Not)

I was hurt for three whole days.

I had never stayed hurt or mad for this long, I knew it was wrong and knew something was going to have to be done.

I walked into the bedroom, shut the door and put my hand up like you do when you are going to stop someone and I said, "I know God, I know what you want me to do, I know what you are going to tell me and I don't want to hear it so I'm not going to talk about it. I'm going to read my Bible but I don't want to talk about.

God didn't say anything so I sat down on the bed and started reading my Bible.

I had been studying the book of Mark so when I opened it up it was at Mark chapter three.

I looked down and read these exact words, "He, (Jesus) looked around at them in anger and deeply distressed at their stubborn hearts."

I quickly closed my Bible.

What was that doing in there?

Why did I have to read about Jesus being distressed over someone's stubborn heart?

Couldn't I just enjoy having a stubborn heart?

I thought back about coming into the bedroom and telling God I didn't want to talk about my bad behavior.

In my mind's eye I saw God and the Holy Spirit standing there sort of like parents do and God told the Holy Spirit, "She won't listen to me, you deal with her."

I guess that's as it should be since the Bible says the Holy Spirit will convict us of sin.

He convicted me and I told God I was sorry and I knew what I had to do.

I got my shoes and put them on and went down to the greenhouse.

I saw all four of the kids looking out Heidi's upstairs bedroom window and they said, "There she goes."

I was ashamed it had taken so long for them to see me go but glad I was going.

I went in and said I was sorry and all was well.

I've never forgot that lesson, I think of it often.

I don't ever want to have a stubborn heart and I'm glad God just plain and simple called me on it when He saw it.

I'm glad He pours grace all over my stubborn heart and softens it up.

I'm glad He saves me from myself.

Did You Ever Know What It Was To Love The Land?

Did you ever know a place so well you could feel it and smell it even when you weren't there?

I have.

I think a farm has a great way of impacting a person that way.

I can still see the farm fields I walked in as a girl.

I can still feel the way the summer heat beat down on the pasture, drying the grass and packing the cow paths.

I can still see the hinges on the fence post that the gates swung on and I remember how it felt in the woods and the way it smelled in the spring, summer, winter and fall.

Not only our farm but my grandparents place as well.

They had a marvelous big barn.

There was a large wooded work bench or table with drawers. There were wooden ladders going to the loft and a wooden peg with feed sack ties hung on it. Lots of burlap bags and pitch forks.

There was a corncrib and a hand corn sheller in it.

The tobacco barn was tall and long and had rows and rows of poles that my uncles climbed up as they hung tobacco.

There was a tobacco press and a long table that the men worked at pulling the leaves off and grading each one.

The cows had a path to the pond and around the top of the bank.

There was a hand pump between the house and the pond and I remember going there with Grandma to get water.

It seems I can remember every detail of the woven wire fence that was outside the kitchen window and behind the grape arbor.

The porch was a cistern top and Grandpa would sit there and smoke his pipe or cigar in the evening.

I can feel it all.

It's crazy how a piece of land or a barn or even a shed can get into you like that.

How you can know and recall every part of it.

Now I hear my kids telling stories about this place, about our barn and our ponds.

They tell about playing in the loft and using sow crates to make playhouses out of.

Climbing trees and scaring each other in the woods.

This place has got into them the very same my childhood home got into me.

There is just something about a piece of land, or a pond or a barn, it is almost like your life blood.

It gets in you and it never leaves.

My dad always told us kids if a man has a piece of land he has something.

I know dad meant he can provide for himself, he has a place to belong, he has roots and a foundation.

I realize more each day how right he was.

I hope somewhere in your past or somewhere in your future you will be blessed to know what it is to love the land.

Summertime is Hay Time

Summertime is hay time.

The old saying, "Make hay while the sun shines" is certainly true isn't it?

All else goes on the back burner when the hay is ready.

Our very first wedding anniversary supper was put on hold because there was hay down and it looked like rain.

Usually the first cutting is before school gets out.

The weather is watched morning, noon and night and when it looks like it's going to be dry the hay comes down.

There is almost no better smell than hay drying in the fields.

We don't see as many square bales as we used to.

It's hard to get the help.

Someone to drive the tractor, someone to stack and someone to pick-up, ideally two to stack and at least a couple of others walking the field but when that can't be pulling the baler with a wagon behind and a man on the wagon will get the job done.

It's a big job to stack a load of hay. There is a right way to do it, a safe way to do it. A well stacked load of hay or straw is not only pretty but something to be proud of.

Then there is the trip to the barn. You sit up on top of that high stack and the breeze feels so good hitting you as the tractor speeds up a little.

The weather reports are saying to stay inside they are saying it's too hot to be out but the farmer doesn't listen.

He not only goes to the blazing hot hay filed but then he goes to the smothering hot hayloft.

How do they take it? I don't know.

My dad says he remembers after he and his brothers left Home his dad bought a hay elevator but before that he and his brothers had to throw them from the wagon to the loft. When the wagon was full it wasn't too bad but as it emptied and got lower the job got harder. One of the few job that gets harder as it goes instead of easier.

Once the elevator is going and the hay is placed on it the motion is started and everyone needs to keep the pace. A hay elevator is a wonderful thing. It makes an already difficult job a little easier.

Just as stacking the hay on the wagon is important so is stacking the hay in the barn. Neatness counts.

The day ends and everyone passes around the thermos of ice water, turning it up and drinking after one another.

Clothes are dusting and covered with bits of hay or straw and soaking with sweat.

Caps are pulled off and forearms are rubbed across foreheads and hands through hair.

Some of the men stand others sort of bend down without their knee touching the ground like you've seen men do and they talk.

They talk about how the hay is, how much they got, how the neighbors hay looks, when they will cut again, how the machinery all worked, about the kind of machinery they would like to have and the kind they used to have.

The talking slows down and finally someone calls it a day.

Everyone heads to their trucks or to the house whichever the case might be and another hay season is either underway or done until the next year.

I don't think there is any other job that follows seasons like farming does.

Well the job of motherhood does, we have seasons with our children as they grow.

Maybe that's why farming and families go so well together, they understand each other, they respect the seasons of life and of nature.

You can't hurry from one to the other, you have to wait for each season to complete its cycle and you have to do what each cycle calls for when it calls for it.

It's the only way, it's just how things work.

Families and farms, no wonder they go so well together.

Let's Talk Stockyards

Let's talk stockyards.

When Mark brought the mail in the other day I looked at the Advantage and noticed an article about the stockyards in a nearby county closing.

They had closed once before but a group of farmers started it back up but now the number of cattle coming in to the yards has dropped again making it impossible to remain open.

When I read this I thought of the Bourbon Stockyards, I recalled making trips there as a child with my father and grandfather.

Do you remember all of those gates, all the noise and all those rats?

I'm thinking back to when we saw so many pickup trucks with racks and not as many cattle trailers.

It wasn't uncommon to see several pickups loaded with livestock heading to the stockyards at any given time.

I also thought about what happened before you left for the stockyards.

The sorting and loading.

The cattle scared me and the hogs annoyed me

If you and your husband have ever loaded hogs together and your marriage survived, then you can make it through anything.

The same is pretty much true for cattle.

Not just for trips to the stockyards but to the locker plant as well.

Once we had a steer to load for the locker plant and we had him in the back of the barn on grain. The day came to load him and Mark had the trailer backed up to the door and went back to let him out.

He looked at me and said, "Now don't let him through yet, he's been penned up and he is gonna want through but don't let him go."

I always hate it when he says stuff like that.

It's one of those no way to win things.

If I hold my ground against the big oncoming steer and it runs over me he will say, "What's wrong with you, why didn't you get out of the way?"

If I step aside to let it pass he will say, "What's wrong with you? Why didn't you stop it? It won't hurt you!"

Finally, after lots of stress the truck would be loaded and the trip to the stockyards or locker plant would begin.

I can still see my Grandpa Marshall, my dad and my uncles loading a big black angus bull. I was so afraid for them. They didn't seem scared at all but I was.

I can remember how he tossed his head and looked through the racks at me.

Mark's Grandpa, Herman raised boars and one of the last York boars he ever sent to Louisville weighed nine hundred and ninety-nine pounds.

That was big but then back then we raised a different type of hog.

Once there you looked at everyone else and what they brought. You notice how your animals look in comparison.

You fill out the papers and sign your name and then we always left for home but first we stopped at Kentucky Fried Chicken in Hamburg.

Then the waiting begins, you look for the check in the mail

You talk about how you will be satisfied with whatever you get then the check comes and often you aren't satisfied but then again you may be very pleased.

It's really just another way farming has changed and we've had to change with it.

Still though you have to admit it would be sort of nice to be crossing the Ohio River bridge look over and see an older man in his overalls, with his cap on, racks on the back of his pickup taking a load of good old fashioned fat hogs to the stockyards.

I wonder if he would stop at the KFC on the way home?

Strawberry Season

It's strawberry time again.

While I love strawberries I admit I hate strawberry patches.

I don't like picking berries.

I don't like weeding berries.

I don't like strawing berries.

I don't like spraying berries after a frost.

I don't like stemming berries or slicing berries or putting them in bags.

I sort of like making jam but other than eating them or giving them away that's about all I like about berry season.

Mark has an obsession with strawberry patches.

He always wants them and he always wants them bigger than they currently are.

He always wants me to want them bigger than they currently are and he always wants me to help make them bigger.

He wants me to make shortcake by making crust, I want to make shortcake by baking a cake.

I think you are beginning to see the problem aren't you?

We're not compatible when it comes to strawberries.

This is a point of contention in our marriage every spring.

Thankfully it only lasts but a short time.

Soon the berries will be picked and in the freezer or jammed in jars.

The new plants will be set, the weeds will be gone and the berries and the contention will both sleep until next spring.

Who knows, by then maybe I will have decided to like weeding and picking and strawing and hosing frost off berries.

The Making of a Farmhouse

Did you ever stop and wonder why a farmhouse is called a farmhouse?

It has to mean more than just a house on a farm, I think it means farm in a house.

If you currently farm or have farmed in the past I think you'll agree.

I mean what other kind of house save a farm house has had several baby calves come in to get warm by the wood stove a time or two?

Baby pigs in a box with a heat lamp, you know the ones that decide to be born on the coldest night of the year.

What about those new baby chicks you picked up at the post office if you went big time and ordered them from McMurry or even if you just picked a few up at the local Tractor Supply or hardware store.

Did you put them in a washtub or large box with a heat lamp and sugar water right there in the kitchen or living room?

Did you listen to them peep all night and everyone gather around to look at them in the morning?

Are there various animal medicines in your refrigerator right now?

Do you have syringes and dispensers, razor blades and cat gut somewhere stored away?

How about this one, an incubator for starting eggs or heat pads and grow lights to start plants?

I've had both of those in my house.

In January we could never use our back door because it would have a table pushed up against it and be covered with heat pads and trays of tomato seeds while heat lamps descended from the ceiling held in place with bailer twine.

There's that trail of "stuff " you find on the kitchen floor because he didn't have time to take his boots off when he came back in to get that drill bit he left on the kitchen counter.

There's a farm calendar on the wall with important dates scribbled in along with planting signs.

Stray parts and tools, nuts, screws, washers, nails, gaskets, gloves, caps and work boots

Today farmhouses are a lot nicer than those of yesteryear and granted a lot less farming takes place inside the house than it used to but there is still that one thing that happens at the close of every day.

The farmer still comes in for the night.

He still has that place where he hangs his cap and takes off his boots.

He has his chair and the little table nearby for his drink, his popcorn, remote control, farm magazines, and the paper.

There are the phone calls about crops and livestock, barns and bills.

The discussion of all he did today and what he wishes they had got done and the plans for the morrow.

It's when all of this is said and done that you know why a house on a farm in called a farm house.

It's more than a house on a farm, it's the farm and the farmer inside the house that makes an ordinary house into a farmhouse.

Springtime on the Farm

What do I love about Spring?

The real question is what do I love about springtime on the farm or maybe the even bigger question is what is there not to love about springtime on the farm?

Just today as I was standing at the sink washing the breakfast dishes I noticed the lilies coming up around the clothesline posts in the backyard.

The Robins are bobbin all over the front yard and I can hear the birds singing.

The field across from the house has a wet spot in it and the geese make it a stopping point every year on their return north. If you step out on the porch just as the daylight is coming you will hear them really carrying on over there. That always gets our farm dogs, Noah and Runt worked up and barking and brings a quick end to any hopes I may have had of sleeping in.

The fields are dotted with new calves, sometimes they are lying in the sun beside their momma's others times they are running and bucking through the field.

While I'm getting dinner I can watch our Amish neighbor plowing his field next to our place with his team of horses' he stops when he gets to the end of the row to rest the team and then starts out again.

The Maple trees all around have the clear plastic bags hanging around them as they have been tapped for sap. The bags grow fuller every day and soon the smoke from the Amish flues in the barns will rise as they start cooking down the sap to get the syrup.

I can be assured I'll find some new kittens in the barn or the greenhouse.

There's always the smell of wild onions too and the faint color coming to the woods as the trees just begin to bud out and then next thing you know the redbuds are everywhere.

The list of things I love about springtime on the farm is endless, there is just no natural stopping place so I guess I'll just stop.

I think I'll just step out on the porch and savor the season.

Why don't you join me?

When you've finished reading this, put the paper down and walk over to the window or out on to the porch.

Look and listen to what all is going on around you, breath in the fresh spring air.

You and I both know it's been a long time coming so savor it my friend, just savor it

Contentment

I remember when Jessica was born I wrote in her baby book that I hoped she would be content.

What a blessing to be a content person.

Content doesn't mean you don't strive for more or that you don't work to make things better, it just means you are happy, thankful and fulfilled where you are and with what you have until and if you move on.

I have been a content person for the most part all of my life.

I remember one time when the want more monster got a hold of me but I caught on to him quickly and threw him out.

We used to rent a house over around Pekin. We didn't have much all of our furniture was used and we finally got to buy a new living room suite from Value City.

I was excited and thought it was beautiful.

I thought it was beautiful until I went to bed anyway.

I could see into the living room from our bedroom and I laid there feeling like I just had to wiggle with excitement when I looked at the new furniture.

I left the lamp on in there because it made it look cozy and made me wiggle more.

Then all of a sudden it occurred to me how much better it would look if I had a new rug to go with it.

I stopped wiggling.

Suddenly it was no longer perfect, in an instant it had become wiggle unworthy.

Nothing in that living room had changed one bit, the couch was still beautiful the lamp still gave a cozy glow.

I had changed, my heart had become discontent.

You know how it is when something happens that helps you learn a lesson? Well, that was one of those times for me. I think of it often.

Fast forward down the road a few years and I caught myself again.

Mark and I were going to go to a hog producer's dinner.

It was like a date for us because we never went out I was so excited.

I wanted a new outfit so badly but there was no money for one.

When we came home that night I thought about it again and realized if I had got one, it would have been an old one after I wore it.

That would mean I would think I had to have another the next time. It would mean I would always be in a constant state of want instead of contentment and thankfulness.

My mom taught me a lot about being content and I used her lessons often.

Like the following story for instance.

Once when the kids were small the bottom fell out of the hog market we went from having a barn full of hogs that were worth a lot to a barn full of hogs that were not worth much.

We couldn't afford to fill our gas tank at the house.

We didn't want to tell mom and dad because they would fill it and we didn't want that so we waited until we could fill it.

In the meantime, I woke one morning really cold and I pulled the cover up around my shoulders and found myself saying, "Thank you God that I have a cover and that I can move my arms to cover myself up."

A picture of my mother flew into my mind.

Because of her example I wasn't there telling myself how bad I had it, I wasn't saying how I shouldn't have to live like that.

I wasn't telling myself Mark should do better by me.

Instead I was pulling up my blanket and thanking God for what he had provided me.

Almost always when it comes to the discontent buttons in our life there is a content and thankful button right beside it.

It's completely up to us which one we decide to push.

Which one we pick makes a huge difference in our lives and the lives of those around us.

Go home tonight and look at all you do have.

Be amazed by it.

Think of where you started and how far you've came.

Think of people who could never dream of living like you do and not about people who live like you can't.

I pray contentment and thankfulness for all of you.

It really is one of the best things to have.

Remember and never forget what the Apostle Paul said in the book of Philippians, "I am not saying this because I am in need, for I have learned to be content whatever the circumstances.

I know what it is to be in need, and I know what it is to have plenty. I have learned the secret to being content in any and every situation whether well fed or hungry, whether living in plenty or in need. I can do all this through Him who gives me strength."

Have a blessed day full of contentment and thankfulness!

Why Not a Media Fast and a Family Time Feast

I know the second week of January is the traditional Media Fast time, but I'm wondering if we shouldn't up that date a little this year.

Why not keep the TV off tonight? Why not keep it off for the rest of the week?

Sometimes things happen that make us sit back and see things for what they really are.

Think of the countless hours spent sitting in front of shows that are a total waste of time.

They don't even promote anything we say we believe.

As a matter of fact, most things we watch we would say we don't agree with.

It gets easy to fall into a rut and not even know we're in it.

Think about it for a minute, stop and go through the day in your mind.

You get up, lots of times the TV comes on, you get the kids up, the TV is on.

If you take them to school, they may watch a movie in the car.

You come home from work, you get supper ready, you eat, you help with homework and the TV could still be on.

Then with whatever time, if any, is left for family time, ends up being TV time.

Something is wrong with this picture.

We all know it but it seems too easy to just keep doing it.

You will never be sorry for the night you shut the TV off and read to the kids.

Pick something small or go ahead a pick a big book that might take you reading a chapter a night for a week or two to finish.

Play games.

Go for a walk around the yard, woods or neighborhood.

Work together on the house or outside, clean out the car, whatever it is do it together.

The kids will protest and you may even want to protest or give up, but don't.

In time you will wonder why you didn't do it sooner.

This isn't to say TV night can't be a fun night or movie night isn't a great thing, I'm just saying we shouldn't let it become our "every night," or what we default to with no thought at all.

You will never ever regret a night not spent in front of the TV but you might look back and regret all the ones that were.

Take a media fast and replace it with a family time feast this week or better yet, for the rest of your life.

You won't be sorry.

Downloaded or Tattered

Every generation seems to have things they watch go along the roadside. Things replaced by newer and better products or ways.

Last night I made supper with the laptop open on the counter so I could prepare an on line recipe. Gone was my recipe book. The ones with missing pages, broken bindings, stained pages from ingredients that missed the bowl and plopped down on the book. Gone was my need to ever buy another bound cookbook.

Then I thought of other books. I thought about my Bible. I thought about how my girls read the Bible from their phones. I thought about how people in church follow along in the Bible by reading from their phone. I realized my need was gone to ever buy another bound copy of the Bible.

My need to buy bound books may be disappearing but my want to isn't. I love books. I love to smell them. I love to hold them in my hands. Somehow the thought of passing down a handwritten book of recipes to your daughters, or a paperback collection of family or community recipes collected and published for a good cause, means more than a download on the computer.

Then I thought of my Bible. I thought of all the tattered Bibles I've seen. The broken down bindings, the pages marked well by use. The pen marks, marking the verses the owner either clung to or rejoiced in. I thought of the Sunday morning sound of all those pages turning when the preacher tells us what scripture to go to. I thought about how I like to hold my Bible in my hands and the life I feel in it. I wondered how I could get that same feeling from a phone or a computer. I don't think I can. My children may be able to but I think it's to late for me. I want my stained cookbook. I admire and honor a tattered Bible.

So while I enjoy the convince and money saving way I can use my laptop for recipes and even scripture, at the end of the day I want a bound copy. A bound copy I can touch with my life, I can spill ingredients on my cookbooks and I can mark my Bible and hold it close until it becomes tattered and worn from doing life with me, and I become better from doing life with it.

Oh For The Patience Of The Ocean

I don't think anything can make you realize things about yourself like the ocean can.

Can anything make you feel smaller? Can anything make you realize how small you are like the ocean can?

With all the things we can do and all the strength we have, no one can stop the ocean. There is no power on earth that can hold it back.

- Who can control the ocean?
- Who can stop its waves?
- Who can fathom how deep and wide?
- Who can know all its secrets?
- Who can number the grains of sand?
- Who can tell the waves to stop?

I stand and look at it and I can't even take it in, I can't comprehend the magnitude or the power of what I'm really seeing. What we consider to be one of, if not the most powerful and uncontrollable things in the world is so easily held in the palm of God's hand. It lies there and waits for His word.

Job 38:8-11 "Who shut up the sea behind doors when it burst forth from the womb?

when I made the clouds its garment and wrapped it in thick darkness, when I fixed limits for it and set its doors and bars in place", when I said, "This far you may come and no farther; here is where your proud waves halt?"

I thought about how strong and mighty the ocean is and yet it lies in God's hand waiting for His word. I thought about how weak and powerless I am and yet I jump out of God's hand, I don't wait for His word and I rush ashore. Time after time I do that.

In my mind I see the ocean and myself lying in God's hand watching the sunrise. I'm the hyper-active one. I see it coming and start getting all antsy. Next thing you know I jump up, weak and frail and ignorant as I am and make a break for my day. The ocean on the other hand, as big and strong and powerful and proud as it is, lies there and accepts God's rule over it.

Oh to be more like the ocean, to have its patience. To willingly and safely wait in God's hand for His word.

Everybody is Somebody

I remember when I was a little girl coming out of the store with mom and she smiled and spoke to someone.

I didn't know the person so I looked up and asked her who it was.

She looked down at me smiling and said, "I don't know, but they're somebody."

I have thought of her answer countless times since then.

She was so right, everyone is someone and just by a smile and a greeting, mom had acknowledged that, and taught me to do the same.

I read a story about a lady who decided when she went to work she wasn't going to smile at, or greet anyone.

She would speak and smile if the other person did it first but she wouldn't be the first.

It didn't take long for her to notice she didn't get a lot of greetings or smiles.

When she didn't smile first others felt a little uncomfortable, they wondered if she was upset or mad at them or worse yet didn't even like them anymore.

The story goes on to tell how we are basically all in need of some sort of acknowledgement from the people we see.

Everyone is waiting to see if someone will think them worthy of a smile or greeting. While we may not realize it or say it out loud we all want someone to notice us.

The lady said she decided from then on she would have a friendly ministry. She would make sure she spoke and smiled first. She would be the one to put the other person at ease and make them feel like somebody.

She would let them know she saw them and she was glad to see them and thought them worthy of her time.

I guess this was on my mind today with all shopping and holiday hustle and bustle.

It makes me want to have a "friendly ministry" of my own.

I want everyone to know they are somebody, somebody that matters to me.

Equal Doesn't Always Mean the Same

Equal doesn't have to mean same.

Two things can be equal but very different.

Take men and women for an example.

Men and women are equal, yet they are not the same, they're very different.

You often hear people say Christianity and the Bible look down on women.

They say Christians hold women down.

All one need do is read God's Word to find that isn't true.

It is true in the Old Testament women were treated badly.

That was never God's plan.

In the New Testament men were treating their wives badly, leaving them for any reason.

Jesus told them to stop it.

He told them to love their wives, to take care of their wives, honor their vows and give their life if need be for their wives.

Remember in the beginning when God created man?

He said man needed a helper.

What does the word helper imply?

It implies there where things he couldn't get done on his own.

You see, Adam was created perfectly, just as the woman was, but he was created perfectly to do what he was created to do.

But he wasn't created to do it all.

So God knew he would need help.

A woman was the answer, she couldn't do everything either but she could do what she was created to do.

Together they could do all that needed done.

It's still the same today.

We don't have to try to be alike to prove we are equal.

Equality is never questioned by God it is assumed by Him.

When we spend all our time trying to prove we are equal we're really just trying to promote ourselves.

We're already equal, different yes, but equal.

Don't waste your time trying to be the same or prove you are equal.

You don't have to.

Equality is a gift bestowed on us by God just like our differences are a gift.

As with any gift it's meant to be enjoyed.

So, don't get caught up in the age old useless chatter.

Know who you are and what you are worth and enjoy the gift of equality.

We All Need a Story

I know I've said it before but I have loved each stage of my life.

Yet I have no desire to go back to any stage other than the one I'm in at the time.

I've just always been that way.

Today I was talking to a young mother who has a little one in diapers and she doesn't have a dryer.

When I was a young mother I used cloth diapers and didn't have a dryer.

I hung diapers up everywhere in the house in the winter and every other kind of clothing article too.

I never even minded much.

It was just the way it was and I did what I had to do.

We drove old cars and older trucks.

We paid our bills and that was about it.

Sometimes we could hardly do that.

Yet, I was always content.

Knowing that, why is it when I hear about a young couple doing that same thing today it grips my heart and I want to rush in and make things easy for them?

Why do I find myself worrying about young couples, feeling bad for them when I know they are having it rough starting out?

I guess the same reason older couples have always had a heart for younger couples.

I know it's good for us to have to work together to make it when we're young. I know struggle and hard work bring a good reward.

I know we all need to pay our dues and I know we have to crawl before we can walk.

So I guess instead of wanting to run out and buy a clothes dryer for every young mother with little ones I should be glad for her to be in the stage of life she is in.

Every stage is a once in a life time kind of stage and we shouldn't miss any of them but instead enjoy them to the fullest.

Later on when we look back at them they will be ten times sweeter than they ever were when we were living them.

I guess what I'm saying is sometimes to take someone's struggle away is to take their story away and we all need a story.

Something to look back on with pride.

Something hard to tell about.

Something to leave us feeling tough and capable.

The young adult life stage is a treasure and the middle age stage is a treasure and I know the older stage is going to be an eye opener too.

I guess to sum it up, life is good and we need to enjoy the struggles and pleasures each one brings.

So savor your season, give a helping hand when you can but don't be to quick to take away a struggle or you may just take away a story of pride and making do and remember, we all need a story.

Bridal Shower Advice and Homemaking Sanity

When I got married in 1983 I was given a bridal shower.

The guests were all asked to bring a recipe. Now it's been almost 30 years and things have certainly changed.

One of the recipes I received was for Smothered Baked Chicken it came complete with instructions on picking the best hen from the flock, killing and dressing method and of course the baking instructions.

I was told not to throw away money on throw aways. For example, after I had a good supply of paper grocery sacks stored up I should cut the extra up and use for grease blotters in my platter of fried chicken instead of wasting paper towels for it.

Of course now we don't get paper sacks at the grocery and frying is taboo.

But I still fry chicken (but I don't dress them myself) and I will still cut up paper bags when I have them.

Another word of advice on being a frugal housewife was when the bath towels become worn I should cut them up for use as washcloths. I still do this too.

Of course there was the wipe off your foil, rinse out your baggies advice too and I still do that today also. Not as much as then but I will still do it.

I remember one of Marks aunts gave us a radio. A transistor radio, it had the wood grain look and I was so proud of it. I can still see where we sat it.

I got a pressure cooker and a cold packer both.

I got a sewing basket although I can't sew.

It's amazing how fast the time goes and how quickly the things a new bride is thought to need and things older women think she needs to know change.

Or maybe it really doesn't change so much. After all, when I look back at my list I see I mentioned I still do several of the things they told me.

Or maybe I'm just not changing.

Whatever the case, time marches on and the work of homemaking has gotten easier than it's ever been.

The stress level in the home may be higher than it's ever been but the actual work load has been made easier.

So take it from this older woman, who learned from even older women, when the stress builds up wield out those pinking shears and chop those paper bags and bath towels to pieces!

How do you think they stayed sane anyway?

Produce, It's Who We Are and What We Do

I've had several questions about the greenhouse side of our life so I thought I'd devote a blog to it.

Now for some of you you've heard all this before so I promise there won't be any hurt feelings if you just skip over this post.

Mark's family has raised produce for as long as anyone can remember.

I'll go back to the 1800's when Marks great grandparents were farming in Polk Township, Washington County, Indiana.

They of course raised produce in the fields with their focus on tomatoes.

Grandpa Herman often shared stories with us about taking the tomatoes by wagon to Louisville, Kentucky to sell at the market there.

This was before the bridges were built and they ferried across.

Sometimes they would stay the night in the wagon along the road.

When Grandpa Herman grew up he married Ruby Fisher, Grandma Gray and they bought a farm in Pierce Township but still in Washington County.

They raised eight children on this farm.

Grandma Ruby said when the kids were little she would sit them under a shade tree near the field when they were really little she tied them in the high chair so they couldn't get away.

She said she would stop, sit under the tree and polish tomatoes for packing while nursing the baby.

Grandma had a farm in Wood Township, that's in Clark County.

I can't remember right now if she bought that place or inherited in but either way Mark's dad and mom bought it from her and that's where Mark was raised.

They started out with field tomatoes too.

Mark and his siblings have lots of stories about working in those fields of tomatoes.

One of Marks favorite stories is about how his mom would come out and blow the car horn when the noon meal was ready.

He said they listened all morning for that horn to echo through that field.

They built the greenhouses in 1976 and are still growing tomatoes today.

Mark's dad, Lowell turned 84 on the second of this month and his mom, June, will be 82 in May and they still grow three large greenhouses of tomatoes each year. This year included.

You would never know they are as old as they are.

In 1987 Mark and I rented one of his dad's greenhouses and had our first crop.

The next year we bought the farm where we live now and Mark got about the business of building our first greenhouse.

We cut the lumber from the place and built our first wood frame greenhouse.

A couple of years later we were able to afford two more metal frame houses so we had a total of three house.

Mark kept working public work for several years leaving me and the kids to tend the greenhouses.

I found myself living Grandma Gray's life.

I watered, suckered, and pollinated tomatoes all with a baby on my hip and little ones around my legs.

So this is the story of how we came to grow tomatoes. It's the story of our people, who we are and what we do.

Remember the Important Stuff This Fourth of July

Today is a busy day full of preparations for the festivities of the Fourth.

We're having both sides of the family to Lost River for supper and fireworks, (if the rain holds off) I'm going to be making some Fourth of July games up just in case we need a backup plan.

There are yards to be mowed and weed eating to be done. Food to make and tables and chairs to set up.

Oh yes, someone is going to need to buy those fireworks.

In all of the busyness I don't want to forget to remember.

I want to remember all those who have gone before me to make today possible.

I want to spend some time thinking all the way back to the Mayflower.

It was a brave man who walked up on that ship headed for a new land and a better life but if possible it was even a braver woman who followed him across that boarding plank while she held the hand of one child and carried another. She had no idea what was ahead or if they would even make it. She not only endured a lot but watched those she loved endure a lot. Think about her today. What she did mattered.

Think about those brave men who signed the Declaration of Independence. When they put their name down on that paper they knew full well they did so at the risk of their lives. Their wives had to be scared. Afraid for them to do it and afraid for them not to. They stood to lose everything but they signed anyway. Remember them today.

I think about years later when men went by horseback and covered wagon to settle the west. They were brave, strong men who had brave strong women at their side. Imagine the thoughts that went through those women's mind as they climbed up in that small buckboard with their little ones on their lap are peering out the back. Just like those ladies before her who boarded that ship, she knew not what was ahead or what this trip would cost her. She had no idea if her family would survive but she went on anyway. Spend some time being thankful for her today.

We've had a Civil War and World Wars.

A Dust Bowl and a Depression.

We've faced Pearl Harbor and Nine Eleven.

We've had inventions and cures.

We've built schools and corporations.

We've church buildings on every corner.

We feed the world.

We have more wealth than any other people on the planet.

We have freedom and safety like very few know.

The men and women who built this country were something.

They had strength, vision and backbone.

They didn't wait for someone to make their way or make the way easier, they put their nose to the grindstone and made their own way.

Live in such a way that if they were allowed a visit back this Fourth of July they would be proud of you. They would think what all they faced had been worth it.

Honor them by working as hard as they did for what you want and need.

Honor them by being brave men and women who live a life of integrity and character, striving to be all you can be and to make the world better.

That's what they were all about.

Think about those things today.

Think about them tonight and tomorrow night as the skies light up with fireworks.

Do your part to make America what they dreamed of it being.

Have a wonderful Fourth of July and oh, by the way, don't forget to stand when Ole Glory passes by in the parade.

Maybe It's Time To Put The Self-Help Books Down

We are so obsessed with ourselves, are we not?

We tell ourselves we have got to love ourselves or we can't love anyone else.

The Word of God tells us we are to love others like we already love ourselves.

We tell ourselves and each other that we have got to believe in ourselves.

God tells us we are to believe in Him.

Not one time in the whole of God's Word do you ever see Him in a conversation with anyone where He says, "You know the problem is you don't think high enough of yourself, you have got to love yourself."

Not one time do you see God encouraging someone for a hard task by telling them they can do it.

He tells them to trust in Him to get it done.

We tell people they need to forgive themselves.

You won't find that anywhere in the Bible.

God tells us to accept His forgiveness.

On the surface all of these things we say sound right.

That's the way Satan always works.

Everything he says makes perfect sense to our human mind.

But God's ways are not our ways, His thoughts are not our thoughts.

The things we tell each other about finding grace, release, forgiveness and happiness are as much of a twist of the truth as what happened in the Garden of Eden.

It's not loving ourselves or in believing in ourselves or in forgiving ourselves that we find peace.

It's in believing what God said and acting on it.

When we act on the Truth, we will find the things listed above, like grace and release and others take care of themselves. They are the fruits of truth.

They can't be gotten any other way.

We have got to love others like we love ourselves, admit how weak and frail and sinful we are, step out of the way and let God work and we have got to accept that His forgiveness reaches as far as the east is from the west.

"Then you will know truth and truth will set you free." John 8:32

So let's put a few of the self-help books down and grab on to the truth of God and experience real love, acceptance and forgiveness.

Sons and the Day They Step Around You

Last night the wind woke me up and so of course when I couldn't go back to sleep I got on facebook.

Cristina, one of my friends had posted that her husband was working and someone pulled in their lane, she went on to describe how she handled everything. She did a wonderful job and all is well but still she longed for the safety she felt when her husband was home.

I know that's true with me.

I always know if something is wrong in the night Mark will take care of it.

One night someone pulled in the lane that goes back to the chicken houses.

The girls and I didn't think much about it because sometimes people think it's a road, they go down, see their mistake and come right back out.

But this time, they went down, turned off their lights and sat there.

Okay, that's when you know you should get your husband, or in this case the girls went and got their dad.

By this time, they had driven up to the barn, which is within talking distance of the house, they stopped and shut their lights off again. We could tell there were three men in the truck.

Mark was standing out on the porch and the girls and I were in the house looking out the door. Lucas wasn't home at all.

Mark hollered out and asked them what they were doing.

They said they were hiding from the police, we could tell they had been drinking.

Mark told them if that was the case he didn't want them on his place and he told them to leave.

One of the men got out of the truck and came across the yard toward Mark, when he got to the porch he reached up like he wanted to shake Mark's hand but Mark didn't shake.

They left, but I was so glad Mark was here to take care of it. It didn't seem to bother him at all, the girls and I were going crazy in the house but he was fine.

Then there was another time we thought someone was down the chicken house lane.

It was really late and we were all in here in the house. Mark opened the door to go down there and Lucas was right behind him.

Something major had happened.

In the past if there was ever any type of danger be it real or perceived Mark was always the first protector, he went I stayed with the kids, I was the second protector.

But this time it was different. Lucas stepped around me, he was going out in front of me.

He was going with his dad.

The line of defense had changed.

My son had become a man and therefore his mother and his sister's protector.

Now it's Mark and Lucas together then me and the girls.

Needless to say no one said anything about it, we just accepted the process but inside my heart was screaming, "Lucas you get back here!"

It is the most beautiful thing, the securest thing and yet the saddest thing when your son steps around you.

You can't pull him back even though everything inside of you screams to.

I know he will forever step in front of me now, he Wouldn't be who he is if he didn't but I'm his momma and I'll forever be trying to push back around and protect him if I feel I need to.

Of course he won't let me, but in my heart I'll always lead the charge...well, right after Mark that is because after all, I wouldn't be a mother if I didn't feel that way.

Fall Brings Brings a Harvest of Security

Everyone loves the fall. There's just something about the harvest.

Springtime brings hope. Hope of a bumper crop. Hope of what might be.

Springtime turns to summer and that's when we tend for the most part find out what kind of hand we have been dealt as far as weather and things. Summer is where the rubber meets the road and often we are made or broken in the summertime. You know what, it just occurred to me, that applies to the seasons of our lives as well as to our crops.

Then there's the fall, fall brings security. We harvest the crops and the gardens. We fill the woodshed full.

We make preparations for the winter and then we stand back and look at the full woodsheds, the lined pantry shelves the bursting grain bins and we feel satisfied, we feel secure. We've done what was ours to do. We've done what we could and it feels good.

How many of you know the feeling you get at the sound of popping jar lids sealing as they cool on the kitchen counter or the beauty of seeing them line your cellar or pantry shelf? I don't know much else that evokes pride in a woman like a shelf full of canned goods. Why I'd say it ranks right up there with a good hair day.

Then there is the woodshed. We know there will come a day when the weather man says bad weather is moving in, snow is on the way but it's okay. We'll feel secure.

We'll feel secure because earlier we had mixed the gas and oil and sharpened the chain and set off for the woods. We cut and we split and we hauled and we unloaded and we stacked and we stood back and looked and we felt secure. We had done what was ours to do.

Let's not forget the crops. You don't even have to be a farmer to get caught up in the thrill and excitement of the harvest, it's sort of contagious.

Who of us hasn't driven down a rural road and saw the combines running side by side, the semi's waiting at the side to be filled or the wagons that run along beside the combines?

What about seeing the farmers standing around a pick-up truck or equipment. They will usually range in age from very young boys to older men. Even though we can't hear them we've heard them before so we know what they're talking about.

They're talking about the equipment, the price, the yield, the neighbors yield, the weather, how long they think they will be able to run.

Then if you watch long enough one of them will bend over and scoop up a handful of grain from the ground or an ear of corn and they'll work it around in their hand they'll get the feel of it, they'll look at it and many things will run through their minds, then they will slowly let it fall through their fingers back to the earth.

The fields will be emptied, we'll be able see our neighbors' farms again, those places in the road we couldn't see around will now be clear.

The crops are in, the bins are filled and we stand back and look and we feel secure.

Maybe that's why there are so many fall parties, hay rides and bonfires.

The harvest is in we've done our work, we've done the part that depended on us, we've met our responsibility and now we can celebrate.

I hope this fall and harvest have found you working, preparing and then leaving you with a feeling of security and a reason to celebrate. I hope there's a hay ride and a bonfire in your future plans.

Savor the season, it will be gone quickly.

A Hand Up

I'm sure you have heard the story of the "Turtle and the Fence Post."

The story teaches the basic principal that if you ever see a turtle on a fence post you know he didn't get there by himself. Someone helped him get there.

The story applies to Mark and I.

Thirty years ago when we started out we didn't have the money to buy a place.

We had money for a monthly payment, but not enough for a down payment.

Mom and Dad loaned us the down payment money to buy the place we now call home.

They told how years ago when they were young my Grandpa, Theodore Marshall, had loaned them money for the down payment on the farm where I was raised.

They paid Grandpa back, we paid them back. My Grandpa helped them up which enabled them to help us up.

I honor my parents today. God used them to give me a home when I was a little girl and again later when I was a grown woman with a little girl of my own, they helped us get our first home.

God blessed the gift they gave back then. Mark the kids and I worked hard together and thirty years later we are blessed to buy another farm. They helped us get the first piece of ground to stand on and then we took it from there.

It seemed only fitting that Dad and Mom should have their picture taken here by the sign. They gave Mark the chance to start a small farm and me the chance to help him.

Thank you Dad and Mom for helping a couple of turtles to see the view from the fence post.

We're forever grateful.

We'll love you always and forever!

What to Get the In-laws for Christmas

What to get the in-laws or more importantly, the mother in law.?

A big question that can really be easy to answer.

If your children are grown, think of the kind of thing you would like to get from them.

If they aren't grown, fast forward in your mind

and imagine it is Christmas 20 years from now and you find a package under the tree from your daughter in law or even son in law, what would you want to find when you unwrapped it?

I asked myself that question.

It might sound self-serving, prideful or even vain, but if it is, I guess I am, because this is what I thought......

I would like a list of all the things they love about my child, things they love that I had taken the time to teach them.

A photo album with notes included of a day I had spent With my grandkids.

It means so much when others take time to love those we love.

A gift card or an outing planned for your in- laws to spend with your spouse alone, just them and their child. If you want to go all out, make it a day for them to spend with all of their children. No in-laws allowed, just mom, dad and the kids, for old time sakes. They will love it.

Make a list of the things you have learned from them over the years, list the things you want to know about them and other things you want to learn.

Make a journal of the Christmas you have had together. Start with that first awkward one when you were dating.

None of these things cost much money put they are priceless.

So go ahead, spread the love and appreciation, it will make your in- laws day!

Besides it will go a long way toward helping you to rise to position of "favorite daughter in law."

Stripping Tobacco at Thanksgiving for Christmas Money

When I was a girl we raised tobacco.

I know tobacco is taboo now but back then it was considered just another crop.

The base was at my grandparent's place.

The tobacco barn sat back in a field behind the house. It was a little distance from the house, barn and other outbuildings.

I remember walking through the pasture to get to it and looking over my shoulder to be sure the cows weren't coming after me. My grandpa had a lot of Herefords and they always scared me a little.

If you've never been in a tobacco barn they are different than you might expect. They're tall and have poles running through them all the way up to the roof where the tobacco is hung on sticks to dry.

There was a long table on one end or maybe both if you had the help and there was sort of what you could call stations at the tables. The leaves of the tobacco were stripped off and the stalk was passed down the line. They were graded as it went down the table. The last stop was what was called the trash, pretty much whatever was left on the stalk. That's the station us kids usually worked the men got the important ones.

My Grandpa, dad and uncles taught us how to hold the leaves and how to tie it off and then put them on a tobacco stick until we had it filled then it would go into a press.

I've watched my uncles climb around all over those barns. They would position themselves at different levels and someone from the ground would pass up a stick loaded with tobacco to the first man, he would grab it and pass to the next one up and so on it went until the barn was full.

I'm reminded of all of this because my dad and brothers always stripped tobacco on Thanksgiving morning. Well, they did if it was in "case" meaning it was damp enough to pull the leaves off without them breaking.

Mom and I stayed home and prepared the meal, really mom prepared and I tasted it.

Later after Thanksgiving but before Christmas the tobacco would be taken to New Albany and sold.

That was our Christmas money.

I remember we got to go out for supper at Kings Table in Clarksville with some of that money. That was a buffet place and considered a nice place at the time.

We don't raise tobacco anymore. Grandma and Grandpa's farm has long since been sold but I'll never have a Thanksgiving or a Christmas that I don't think about that tobacco patch, and barn and the sound of my Grandpa, dad and uncles talking and laughing or maybe even getting mad sometimes. Teaching us kids, smiling when we did right and correcting when we did wrong. It was a part of life, life on a farm and it was good.

As always, I find myself thankful on this Thanksgiving Eve for those memories of my family.

The American Farmer and Thanksgiving

Regardless of what people say the oldest profession is farming.

When God created Adam and Eve and placed them in the garden He instructed them to care for it.

From the very beginning of time men have been farmers.

Not only from the very beginning of the world but even from the very beginning of our country.

No matter where man finds himself one of his first priorities has to be to feed himself, thus farming was always first.

Farming doesn't only mean tilling the soil and milking the cows. It's so much more than that so much wider.

The pilgrims planted and did what they knew how to do and the Indians showed them how to work this American soil, how to feed it and make it productive and they showed them what grew best here.

Then there are farmers of the sea, men who harvest from the ocean and seas.

Hunters that harvest from the woods and fields.

All of these different type of foods would have been present at our country's first Thanksgiving. Someone did all of the different things listed above to put the food on the first Thanksgiving table.

Then they gave thanks, thanks to God for providing for them, they were grateful for the Indians who taught them new things. Thankful for the soil that brought forth it's bounty, they were thankful for the woods and the sea that offered up their goodness to them.

While everything is different today, when you look deeply you will see that nothing is different today.

Even though we're not as aware of it as the pilgrims were our most basic need, or first need is food.

Just as the farmers, the hunters, the fisherman and others made the first Thanksgiving possible they still make it possible today.

When we sit at our Thanksgiving tables we need to remember that every single thing we put on our plate had it's start on a farm.

The turkey and the ham were cared for by a farm family, the corn and potatoes came from a farm, if you have seafood a man when out and harvested it for you. Maybe you'll have deer or quail that came from the woods or even a persimmon pudding from the persimmons you or someone else gathered up.

Without the bounty of the soil, the woods and the sea there would be no thanksgiving. The day was set aside to give thanks for the provisions that were provided.

While we need to remember the American farmer on Thanksgiving Day we can rest assured the American Farmer knows where the real bounty comes from.

He knows his limitations, he knows while he can till, plant, weed and fertilize, the fisherman can cast his nets and the hunter can enter the woods without the grace of

God, without God sending the sunshine and the rain, the heat and the cold there would be no harvest, no harvest of any kind.

Thanksgiving reminds us of how our basic needs don't change, it can even humble us as we stop and really ponder how quickly our nation or any nation can be brought to their knees without food, without a harvest.

One good season doesn't promise another good one. We've got to be ever thankful and be good stewards of the land, woods and sea that God has provided for us.

Take time to look at each platter or bowl on your table this Thanksgiving, think of the farm, the field, the woods or the sea it was harvested from, think about the harvester then join them in giving thanks to the one who make it all possible and feeds His children.

Genesis 8:22 "As long as the earth endures, seedtime and harvest, cold and heat, summer and winter, day and night will never cease."

Happy Thanksgiving!

Healthy Holiday Giving

There's something that's been on my heart for a long time now.

Something I want to share but at the same time I'm a little afraid to share.

Afraid of being misunderstood or having you think I'm saying something I'm not saying or even thinking I'm hard-hearted and selfish.

With Christmas coming and all the giving opportunities we have I can't help but look around at where our society is and wonder, have we given to much.

Maybe it's not that we've given to much but maybe given for the wrong reasons, maybe selfish reasons and in the end we may have caused more harm than good.

It makes us feel good to give so we do. We like to help people who we think need it, but what if we help to much.

What I mean is this, do you know the verse in the Bible that says, "Better a dry crust eaten in peace than a house filled with feasting and conflict?" (Proverbs 17:1) I'm not talking about the conflict part of this verse but the dry crumb part.

I'm saying maybe sometimes it's better to let a man have a small Christmas that he and his family can afford than to run in and take their Christmas over.

Maybe it's better for a child to learn that sometimes there won't be a lot but what we have we worked for. Maybe it gives them the gift of pride and self-worth.

Please understand I'm not talking about cases of dire need I'm talking about a case where a family may only to able to give one or two gifts to their children and we think that's terrible.

The truth is it's not terrible.

Many of us were raised that way or with even less, but listen to the stories that go with those times. You don't have to listen long to hear the pride and the character that was built.

Our wonderful time of plenty has clouded our vision. It's made it easy for us to help so sometimes we reach out to help but when we stand back and look we see while we wanted to give we have stolen.

We've stolen a family's sense of pride, maybe even their thankfulness and contentment.

Again, please don't hear what I'm not saying, I am not against giving at all but I am saying we might want to take another look at how we give.

We may want to work on praising a family for doing what they can and providing the kind of not only Christmas, but clothes and warmth and food for their family that they can with the work of their hands and sometimes that takes the whole family working together and that isn't a bad thing.

So many of the things that give people the grit and integrity we admire we're quick to want to take then we have seminars and meetings on how to fix our society's problems.

Again, I'm not saying don't give but let's not steal either.

Let's not give to the point that we weaken those we want to help.

There are harder things in life than a lean Christmas Tree, actually when you think about it a lean Christmas Tree can turn into something much more beautiful than a fat one.

I say all of that to say this, while you are looking for families to help this year remember there are more ways to help than one.

Encourage and praise the family that you see doing what they can with what they have, while we do need to help one another and be there for one another we do no one a service when we're to quick to always remove their struggle.

We steal their story when we do that and like I've said Before we all need a story of "I remember when" to look back on and tell.

It's where our character is made so maybe if we think we need to see more character today we need to slow down on taking every one's hard time from them.

Maybe that's the best gift we could give.

I can say this because there was a time when my family was a family that you would have thought needed help.

Things were hard for us. The bottom had dropped out of the hog market and what was a barn full of money one day wouldn't pay the bills the next.

We struggled but we made it, now things are better. We have a story. Our children have a story.

Now, if and when they marry and struggles and hard times come they will know how to get by, they have lived through it.

They will know that if you have to shut the heat off in all the rooms save one and you all sleep in the one room that's the warmest and you are the one paying for the heat in that one room it's not a bad thing.

They will know how to be thankful for one room they can heat instead of the others that they can't. They will get up and work every day doing what's before them to do and one day they won't be shutting rooms off.

They will have worked through the hard times and they will have been earned the gifts of grit and integrity.

Make sure that your giving isn't just giving for the good feeling make sure it is giving with a good return.

Make sure you are really helping a person up and not keeping them down.

Again I'm all for healthy giving and sharing of what we've been blest with so Happy healthy giving to all of you.

Dream Tree

When I was a little girl we always had a real tree.

Dad would go cut it off the farm. You know the routine.

It would never stand up straight. We put it in a bucket with sand or rocks and tied it to the curtain rod.

We have put props under the stand and all the other things you no doubt did too.

Remember how when you put the ornaments on an old cedar tree the whole branch drooped?

Yet we thought it beautiful didn't we?

Somewhere Christmas trees became almost a status symbol type thing.

We started having theme trees. Bear trees, Bird trees, bow trees, you name it we made a tree for it.

I went through a time when I wanted one of those trees. I wanted a tree like I saw so many others have. I thought them beautiful.

I still do. I love white lights but Mark and the kids love colored lights so colored lights it is.

Our tree is beautiful and I guess it is a theme tree. A family theme tree.

I don't have ribbons or bows, but you won't believe what I do have.

My tree has 4 empty shot gun shells with a plastic cord hook. Two yellow ones and two red ones.

I have a long rusty bolt with nuts and screws of various sizes on it and you hang it with a piece of binder twine.

We used to always let the kids get a new ornament every year when we went to cut the tree, so I have sponge bob and Grinch.

I have tea pots and unicorns. Santa's, snowmen and angels.

I have a replica of Mark, me, and each of the kids.

I have a little angle my grandma Marshall gave me.

Tonight Jess and Liv have gone shopping to buy new trees for the other place.

They sent me pictures and told me to choose. They called and described real sets of ornaments to me and told me about the white lights.

They told me to tell them what I wanted.

I didn't know what to say. For years I have quietly thought, "one day I will have white lights, I will do the tree with bows and ribbons and bears and bows."

Now is my chance, I get to say what goes.

You know what I ended up telling the girls?

I told them I would like whatever they liked. I told them to make the tree whatever they wanted it to be.

Think of all those years I wasted thinking of the "dream tree" I would one day have.

I guess when the girls called tonight, I woke up and realized I've always had the "dream tree."

Christmas Cards

We got our first Christmas Card yesterday.

Christmas cards have always been one of my favorite parts of Christmas.

It is one of those old fashion, time consuming things I find precious.

When the kids were small I used to always get the cards and have them ready to send out the weekend after Thanksgiving.

We would all sit around the table, each person had a pen or pencil and we would pass the cards around each person signing their name.

We would go down the list and someone would pick a card for the family on the list, sign and pass.

Most of the time this went well, but if we did to many at a time, an argument would break out about someone taking too long to sign or the card choice was poor or someone wrote something embarrassing on the card.

Mark was usually the one guilty of this charge.

I always got inexpensive cards but I remember the year things starting looking up for us. The kids and I went to the Hallmark store in Bedford and bought Hallmark Cards!

They each picked out a box. That was our high cotton year. Makes me laugh now to think of it.

Sometimes I will get a box of nice cards but mostly just plain cards.

My brother always makes the Christmas cards for our parents. He designs a different one each year.

I know postage has gone up but you can send someone Christmas cheer and blessings in the form of a card and for all of less than 50 cents someone will come to your mailbox, pick it up and deliver it for you.

When you think about it, it is really quiet a deal.

Sometimes I send cards with the Christmas message, sometimes old fashion ones, sometimes Santa's and Snowmen, and sometimes animal or even funny ones.

I don't ever put return addresses on my cards.

If I get a Christmas card with a return address I try not to look at it. I want to be surprised when I open the card.

Crazy I know, but it makes it sorta like I get to open a surprise Christmas present every day.

The best part of the card is the handwritten part.

Come on, you know you look to see what your loved one or friend wrote before you read the printed part.

Just knowing someone took time to wish you and your family a blessed Christmas and jot you a note is one of the best gifts ever.

They say Christmas cards are becoming a thing of the past.

They say people are to busy for them.

I hope that isn't true.

Some things we should just never get to busy for.

My vote is Christmas cards are one of them.240

The Nativity Scene, The Root of Christmas

When I was a little girl, Mom always put our Nativity scene under the tree.

I never really wondered why it was under the tree, or you could say at the base of the tree. It just seemed like that was where it belonged.

I used to do that too, but over the course of time, mine has found its way to various tables in the house.

Just this morning I heard something that told why under the tree could be the best place for it.

Christmas isn't about the tree or the gifts. It's about the baby in the manger.

He's the foundation, the root of the whole thing.

So it seems only fitting for Him to be at the base of our tree, tying everything about the season together for us.

Thank You Jesus.

The Old Hymns of Christmas

Glory to God in the highest, And on earth peace, good will toward men.

When the kids were small one of the ways we tried to keep Christ in Christmas was singing.

We would shut all the lights off in the house except the ones on the Christmas Tree then we would all lay down around the tree with hymn books and sing Christmas carols.

If you don't have a hymn book, I'm sure you can find them for free or very cheap since most churches are using screens these days.

There is just something sweet about teaching your child to sing the old Christmas carols from those books.

Even when they can't read the words you can take their little fingers and show them how to move them across the page, back and forth and up and down, as you sing.

Their little voices sound like angels singing and you'll be reminded why Jesus said, "Let the little children come unto me."

And maybe even have a better understanding of why our Lord and Savior came to us first as a babe wrapped in swaddling clothes.

"They were praising Him and saying, "Glory to God in the highest." Luke 2:13

The old Hymns of Christmas are still the sweetest.

The Blessings of a Country Christmas

There's something about neighbors at Christmas time.

When I was growing up mom and dad would fix up boxes of meat to give to the neighbors.

I can still see my dad standing at the washing machine with a box on top of it filling it with meat.

I loved watching him do that.

We raised our own meat and did our own butchering so I don't think we had any concept of the cost of the gift, but it wouldn't have mattered, we would have done it anyway.

Bob and Sandy King were neighbors down the road until they sold their farm and moved to Martinsburg. She brought us the most beautiful sweet rolls I've ever seen. She was a wonderful baker. I still remember how I felt that night when dad opened the door and there was The King family, with Christmas Bread in tow.

Later after Mark and I bought this place it was the same here.

Neighbors would come and bring, jams, jellies, home-made bread and candy, Deer Jerky maybe a Christmas flower or other things.

Sometimes it would be just a card in the mailbox.

Other times there was no tangible exchange, just the gift of looking down the road and seeing their light and knowing they would come at a moment's notice.

The security of knowing someone was there.

That's the best gift there could ever be, that's the blessing of a country Christmas.

GOD OPENED MY EYES

Sometimes the more blessings we have the harder it is to see them.

Sometimes the very fact that we have so much makes it hard to be thankful.

I know I've shared this before but it seems a good time of year to share it again.

Our water here at the house has never been very good so for years we went to Mark's mom and dad's house and hauled our drinking water from the spring.

Good, clean spring water.

Years went by and we built the chicken houses which meant we dug a new well.

Now that water was good, it didn't smell and it had a good taste.

So we no longer had to drive to Pekin to get water, now we just had to walk down to the chicken houses.

I didn't even have to go get it.

That was one of the jobs the kids had, to keep water at the house.

That wasn't good enough for me though.

I clearly remember the day I went to the sink to get water and got mad because I wasn't like everybody else and able to simply turn on my faucet and get a drink.

Oh. I could turn on the sink to get water to wash the dishes or many other things but I couldn't drink it.

I was standing there being mad when all of a sudden I got a picture in my mind.

I know it was God getting my attention.

As I stood there at the sink I saw in my mind those pictures you see on TV of a mother walking five miles with a jug on her head to get dirty water to take home for her children and it will more than likely make them sick.

I saw God looking down at me and God looking down at her.

I felt awful.

We all know how it is to see an ungrateful person.

A complaining person.

I knew how God must feel when he had given me a clean well, just a couple hundred feet from the house, and since he had also given me four healthy strong children I didn't even have to go get the water.

We are such a nation of complainers and one of the reasons is we compare ourselves to each other's massive wealth.

Yes, massive wealth.

If you live in America, you have massive wealth.

If we could learn to see what we have in light of what the world has instead of what our neighbor has or the people in the big fancy subdivision have instead of complaining, we would be completely humbled and awe struck at the magnitude of what we have.

If you go to the store today and you find yourself wanting to get angry at the long lines, imagine yourself in another country.

Do you ever really look at the bounty on the store shelves or do we take it for granted?

Imagine no store to go to.

Imagine if there was a store there were empty shelves \ or full shelves but you had no money to buy anything.

Imagine that you had nothing and there was no Red Cross, no Salvation Army, no government programs, no churches to help you.

That is the reality of what most people live with every day.

Purpose now that when you are in the line at the store you won't complain you will see it for what it really is and not let Satan steal your joy by making you think what is a good thing is really a bad thing.

The fact that you are standing in line is a testament to just how good we have it.

You drove a car to the store, you got out and walked in, you have a huge selection, you can afford to buy what you need and if you can't afford

it there are ways to get help.

When you run out of counter room or table room and you want to complain, stop and think about what you are really saying, listen to yourself.

What you are really saying, is "Oh God, you have given to much, this is just a lot of trouble, I'm not happy about all I have."

We don't think we're saying that but it's what we're saying.

Why not say, 'Wow our table overflows or cup really does run over.

When the house gets so crowded and you want to start thinking about you could use a bigger house look around at all of those faces and think Wow, so many people to love, my house is busting at the seams with love.

Keep people in other places ever present to your heart.

We're weak and we tend to be ungrateful and sometimes we need to clear our minds and wipe our eyes so we can see clearly.

So every time you feel yourself wanting to complain, stop and ask God to show you the truth, ask him to open your eyes and you will find yourself giving thanks instead of complaining.

Oh and just to show you how good God is and how he was really just blessing me before my time I now see that I was just ahead of the game.

I was into bottled water long before it was cool.

Go Ahead, Turn Loose, They'll Make It

This topic came up at one of our Bible studies so I got to thinking about it decided to share some thoughts.

It seems there are always questions about parenting and when our children become teens and make the transition to being adults sometimes it seems harder.

We're at that stage now.

Our kids are pretty much on their own living their own lives.

So here are a couple of things older wiser people told me and I have tried to abide by a lot of it.

First, love who your children love.

An elder in the church once told me that since the time their children had been very small they prayed for the people they would marry and they also determined that they would love whoever their children married.

There is a lot to that.

They may not be who you would have picked.

They may not be as handsome or pretty or smart or spiritual or financially stable as you would like but if they love them we must love them too.

If it is truly a bad choice, we will cut off any opportunity we may have to help or influence if we don't first love.

Secondly, once they reach the mid to later teens or so, they already know what we believe so we don't have to keep telling them.

They have been hearing it for years.

They will have taken it or they won't.

Or maybe they won't take it until later but there comes a time depending on the child's make up when we just have to be still.

Now, this isn't to say there aren't times we will need to speak up but it is going to have to start being less and less.

Third, we have to let them go.

You can't continue to call the shots for them.

You have to see them as the men and women they are and respect that.

Don't call them, let them call you.

Don't give advice.... listen.

If they ask give advice but not a lecture.

Be honest with yourself, go back to your youth.

You loved your mom and dad you respected them and wanted to honor them but there came a time you just had to move on.

Even now we all know how it is when our moms and dads start over parenting us.

What do we do?

We tune them out.

What makes us think ours won't do the same?

There comes a time you have to set them free,

If we don't let them go, they will be forced to push away.

I don't call my kids very often,

I let them call me.

I don't go to their houses unless I'm invited.

I let them come home.

I don't ask a bunch of questions.

I let them tell.... well okay, I'm working on this one.

The point is let's not rob them of the time of being young and excited and ready to take on the world.

Let them make their way, let them write their story.

Some of it will hurt but years later it will be the hurtful, hard parts they will treasure most.

It will be what makes them into fine young men and women and what will put the backbone in a marriage and the strength in a family.

So step back and let them go, besides after all these years, you probably need to go take a nap anyway.

It's okay, go ahead, turn them loose, they will make it.

The Comfort of a Bible

My two favorite Bibles. The green one has my heart but when

the pages starting falling out, I got the pink one and now it's stealing my heart.

Marybeth lost her mother recently and posted on my facebook page how she had been having sad dreams about her mother and when she told her husband about it he said she should place her Bible under her pillow. She said she did and it helped.

Once I was at Bible study with my friend Bobby and she told of a time earlier in her life when she was going through a hard experience.

She said she would just lie in bed at night holding her Bible to her chest.

She just needed to feel it close to her.

I knew just what she was talking about.

I love my Bible and I've often found myself just needing to hold it close.

I've always been impressed with all the pretty Bible covers or jackets I see so many have.

They look so nice and organized and so I've bought a couple different ones and attempted to use them.

Needless to say I never could.

I don't know what it is about me but I just have to have my hands on the Bible, I want to know the feel of it.

I remember one of the Elders in our church standing up before us teaching and I couldn't help but notice how his Bible fit his hand.

It was like a glove, that leather had made contact with his hands so often it just knew what to do and where to fall open.

It was beautiful.

I've always wondered why is it that we get comfort just from holding our Bible?

Then when I was studying the book of John the answer was there.

This is what it says in John 1:1-2 In the beginning was the Word, and the Word was with God, and the Word was God. He was with God in the beginning.

Who is this talking about? What is it saying?

Who is the He it says is the Word?

Look at it again, He is Jesus, He is the Christ and He was with God in the beginning.

That's the answer, that's why we get so much comfort from holding our Bibles.

Our Bibles are the Word and the Word is God, the Word is Jesus.

It's the closest thing here on earth that we have to Him.

In a way it's like when we hold our Bible's we are holding God.

When we know our Bible we know our God.

Now, I know why I draw strength and courage from letting my Bible become one with my hands and my heart.

I know why it gets smudged and the leather gets broken and the pages get torn and bent.

The book of Hebrews says the Word is alive and active and it is.

It's alive and living and doing life with me and thus the smudges, bends and torn pages.

An older lady who I loved dearly told me once years ago, "Honey, even a good life is a hard life."

How right she was, and how glad I am I have the Word to go through life with after all remember that verse in Matthew eleven that goes like this, "Come to me, all you who are weary and burdened, and I will give you rest. Take my yoke upon you and learn from me, for I am gentle and humble in heart and you will find rest for your souls."

Think about a yoke you've seen hanging in a barn, think of how they are dirty and bent and stained with sweat and you might even find some hair still in them.

They started out new and crisp and tight but when they had spent many days with a horse they got to showing signs of wear, signs of doing life.

It's the same way with our Bibles

The verse doesn't say we won't have burdens to bear if we walk with Jesus, or that we won't have to submit to some type of yoke.

It's just the opposite.

Jesus is basically saying, I have a yoke, it's been fitted just for you, no one else. Don't worry you can handle it, I've seen to it.

Can't you almost see Him coming over to you and lifting the ill-fitting yoke you have put on yourself, he is gentle because He knows while you were trying to wear the wrong one you were blistered, cut and wounded.

Imagine Him smoothing salve over the places rubbed in your back.

Then imagine yourself standing still and kneeling before Him while He places His yoke, His will for your life on your back.

Imagine the sigh of relief.

This is what you were meant for.

You can do it!

His Word is alive and it is life giving and it brings comfort and courage like nothing else.

That's why we find comfort in the Bible.

Riding the "Find Myself" Merry Go Round

Sometimes we just get to caught up in things.

Sometimes we take a thought and wear it out.

Take the thought, "I need to find myself."

I know that can have a good meaning, I know there is a slice of truth to it.

I also know we have gone crazy with it and made it way too big of a deal.

We hear people say things like, "I'm more than my husband's wife, or my children's mother or my parent's daughter."

They say they don't want to be defined by their job or where they live or where they are from.

Sometimes that thought sends them on a journey that has no end

At the end of our life nothing will have mattered more to us than being the wife of our husband or the mother of our children or the daughter of our parents.

Even our daily work will seem of significance.

Truth be told we are a part of our work, it is a part of us.

To a large degree there is nothing wrong with that, it's just the way it is.

So take some time to find out what you like and what makes you tick but don't let yourself get caught up on the merry-go-round of "finding yourself."

It's a ride that never stops and if it did when you got off you would find you were still your husband's wife, the mother of your children and the daughter of your parents and your life work would still be there.

And no matter how the world tries to twist it or make you discontent with that, it's true and it's beautiful.

Enjoy who you are today.

No one else can be who you are, that's the secret, that's the ticket.

You see that's the real quest, we all pretty much already know who we are and it is defined in a lot of ways.

We just need to step up and into being the best of who we are.

If you need to put something down that's holding you back, put it down, if you need to step it up a notch step it up.

Then just get about the business of being the best you, you can be.

"I praise you because I am fearfully and wonderfully made, your works are wonderful, I know that full well." Psalm 139:14

THERE IS JUST SOMETHING ABOUT A DOG

There is just something about a dog.

When we were kids we had a German Shepherd.

His name was Tippy.

I was always a little afraid of him although he never gave me cause to be.

As a matter of fact, he was very protective of my brothers and I.

Once my dad was going to give my brother a spanking in the yard and Tippy got after him so Dad rethought it.

I remember we had a man combining once and his combine caught on fire and he was coming off of the combine and Tippy started in after him and he climbed back up on the burning combine.

He never liked the man who delivered our coal and he really didn't like men in general.

Once we had a tobacco base leased at a neighbors and when we went to work there Tippy followed along.

They had a German Shepherd as well and it was white.

Tippy and their dog, King got in a fight.

Now granted we were the visitors and Tippy was the one who didn't belong there and I acknowledge that right up front.

When the dogs started to fighting the owner of the other dog, a woman started yelling, "Kill him King, Kill him.

I was a little girl but I remember that.

I was scared and I can still see that lady in my mind she was all into it and I knew it was wrong to be saying that.

I was just a girl and I knew our dog was the one that didn't belong but I also knew we would have never hollowed out such a thing.

We were concerned for both dogs.

Dad took care of the dog fight and we took our dog home.

Mom and Dad talked about it and I learned a lot from listening. I learned a lot about being a neighbor.

Once, Mark, the kids and I had a Blue Heeler, we got him at the pound and he was the best dog ever.

We named him Bear but we pronounced it Bar.

When the kids were little we would ride back in the field in the truck to see the cows and he would follow along with us he would jump up in front of us snapping at flies or bugs or what have you.

Then he got to where he wanted to bite the tires while Mark was driving.

One day the kids and I were working in the greenhouse and Mark left, it wasn't long before he was back and as soon as he came in the greenhouse I knew something was wrong.

He had ran over Bar and killed him.

Mark cried and we cried.

We buried him in the back yard.

We didn't have many dogs after that but Mark roofed a house and a man had a Beagle dog and he gave him to Mark.

We named her Mimi.

Mark hated that.

He said a man should not have to go to the vet and say out loud that his Beagle dog was named, "Mimi."

Mimi had Runt. Runt's dad was the neighbor's dog.

Then we got Noah, Heidi's Chocolate Lab.

They are both getting old now and this winter is going to be hard on them.

Then Foxey came.

Liv picked her out on line and we went to the airport to get her.

Now that was a major deal for us, you see we just aren't the sort of people who pay for a dog and then drive all the way to Louisville, Kentucky to pick it up at the airport.

But we are those kind of people now.

We love Foxey in a way I would have thought was crazy until we became crazy.

Then Jessica got Charlene and she was so funny and cute but she died in the summer and now Jess has Lucy Lou.

She called and face timed with her dad tonight so he could watch Lucy play.

When Olivia is here and Lucy hears her talking through the phone she jumps at the phone.

Long story short, dogs play a big part in our lives don't they?

Almost everyone has a story about a dog,

They protect us and comfort us and they love us no matter what.

As I was typing this, Lucas came downstairs and looked out on the porch to see Foxey sleeping in a flowerpot, he opened the door and told her to come in.

Now she is sleeping in the foyer without a care in the world.

She is fat, furry, healthy and happy.

I can't help but think as I look at her lying there that just like I said before,

There is just something about a dog.

What Not To Buy Your Children For Christmas

I know we haven't had Thanksgiving yet but I also know the reality of it is many are already doing their Christmas shopping.

After watching television for a little bit I had a thought, I thought about the things we shouldn't buy our kids for Christmas.

Have you noticed the toy or educational commercials lately?

Have you really listened to or looked at them?

I am always struck with the picture they give.

Now first of all don't read what I'm not saying, I don't think there is a thing wrong with a child being able to entertain themselves, I think it is an important thing to learn but I also think as humans we are prone to go to far one way or the other.

We all have to agree we live in a time that is different from any in history.

We spend less time with our children than any parents before us.

Truth is that means we have less time to speak into their lives than any parents before us.

We have done this so long we have lost sight of what we are doing.

We see commercials that show us a little one sitting alone in the living room playing with her toy/computer that is teaching her to read.

Her mother peaks around the corner to see her, smiles and goes back to what she is doing and the child is alone.

We buy snuggle blankets because it's a fact a little baby needs snuggled, but because we're so busy we buy a blanket to do it for us.

Now there is a time that those things are okay but the danger is we let them take over and it breeds selfishness in us.

It gets easy to let a toy teach our children or a blanket snuggle them so we can facebook or text or cook or visit or whatever we want to do.

Be aware of the things you buy this Christmas.

Buy things that will promote togetherness.

Buy toys that will get you on the floor playing with your babies, a blanket that will begin to smell like you because you spend some time each day just sitting snuggling your baby in it.

We have got to stop delegating our parenting to teachers, coaches, sitters, daycare and grandparents, and even toys and entertainment.

So back to the point, when you shop this year, shop for family items, buy things that will unite your family, not separate it.

We have got to guard out family time, we can't keep giving it away.

The title of this blog was "What Not To Buy Your Children For Christmas", but maybe we should end it with a question.

Maybe we should ask, "How Will You Spend Time With Your Children This Christmas?"

Don't give the time away to a toy or anyone else.

Start a list today, not a to buy list or a stressful to do list, just a loving list, a list of little ways you love.

It's the best gift you will ever give for them and for your-self and it will be what they tell about when years from now the conversation turns to Christmas' of long ago.

Stop Talking and Start Doing

Let's stop saying that the family is falling apart and let's work on our marriages.

Let's stop thinking we would be happier with someone else or that we don't love each other anymore or that we've out grown each other instead let's grow up, be men and women and protect our marriage and our family.

Let's stop saying today's youth don't know how to work or to show respect.

Instead let's start showing respect to officers, teachers, neighbors, children, parents, spouses and ourselves.

We don't need to say how kids don't want to work anymore, we just need to stop giving them everything. Instead of complaining how we have to do everything and they don't appreciate anything, stop doing and start letting them become men and women.

We can stop saying the morals of the country have gone down the tubes any day now.

We can start living what we say we believe and things will turn around on their own.

It's not the other family, it's not the other people, it's not the other person, it's me and it's you and its time for us to get over ourselves and grow up.

They Grow Up Fast

Mark was sitting out on the front porch talking to Mike on the phone.

They were talking about heifers, trucks, changing the oil and stuff that brothers talk about.

Heidi and Paul pulled in and Mark told Mike he needed to go because he wanted to hold Ezra.

Mike said, "Yeah, you better. He will be a day older tomorrow."

Mark said, "That's right" and with that they hung up.

Between the two of them they have raised nine children so they know how fast they grow and every day counts.

They Are Always Learning

So many times I wish I had a camera.

This morning at church Ezra was sitting on Mark's lap.

Communion was passed and I held the tray for Mark since he was holding Ezra.

Mark had one arm around Ezra and took the communion cup with the other hand, he lifted the cup and threw his head back like men do and drank it.

Ezra stopped moving and tilted his head back until his head was resting all the way back on Mark's arm. He was watching everything Grandpa was doing.

He watched him put the cup back in the tray and then he looked back up at Mark and Mark looked down at him.

An age old scene was being played out again.

Little ones watching, wondering and learning.

He is to little to ask, what Grandpa was doing but he is still learning and still watching.

Playing in the Dirt

I went out on the front porch and Mark was letting Ezra play in the dirt in the flower pots.

I told him he shouldn't be letting him do that.

He said, "Oh Grandma this kind of weather makes a man want to get in the dirt."

What could I say?

I went back in the house and left them to their farming. :)

The Kitchen Table, One of Your Greatest Allies

Today for dinner we had Poppy Seed Chicken, Mashed Potatoes, Baked Beans, Tossed Salad, Rolls and an Orange Sawdust Jello and of course Sweet Tea.

My Grandparents Marshall always feed whoever was at their house, be they visitors or hired hands.

We do the same today.

There's always someone here to eat and I like it that way.

Today while I was getting dinner I got to thinking back over things.

While I made the Sawdust Salad I thought about another salad.

When I was young it seemed at every dinner someone would bring orange jello with carrots and pineapple in it.

Do you all remember that?

I hardly ever see it anymore.

I guess we've got more fancy Jello salads to take the place of that one.

I remember when the men, meaning my dad, grandfather and uncles were working in the fields, or cutting wood or butchering my mom, grandmother and aunts would get dinner.

When the men came in for dinner, they would wait in line to wash their hands and faces and comb their hair before they went to the table.

None of the women or any of us children ate when the men ate.

I can still feel how it was when the men had been served and left to go back out.

My grandma, aunts and cousins would all sit down and eat and I remember it feeling light hearted, I can hear laughter as we ate. It was like the work was done and now they could enjoy their labors.

I can see my aunts standing against the wall or at the stove, sink or table ready to refill serving bowls or meat platters or iced tea glasses.

I remember thick sliced garden fresh tomatoes, crispy fried chicken, and of course milk gravy.

One time, and I think of this so often, unexpected company showed up.

My aunt Katherine was doing the cooking that day and they were asked to stay to dinner.

Aunt Katherine quickly and quietly broke all the ears of corn in half, making it appear as if we had twice as many as we did.

I took a note from her that day, you can always feed a guest one way or another.

I don't know what it is about meal time but it unites people like little else can.

It seems if you share a meal at someone's table they become a friend.

You all know how I am about the kitchen table and I know you're thinking there she goes again and I guess I am.

The kitchen table and what it represents means more than words can express.

It's a feeling. It's a security. It means a sense of belonging and having a place.

Take time to look at your table tonight. It doesn't matter if it's in a kitchen or a formal dining room.

Its job is the same.

It's responsible for bringing the family together, it waits while each one finds their place.

It notices when someone's gone and it rejoices when a guest shows up.

Make it a goal to treasure and respect your table for what it means to you and the well-being of your home.

It's one of your greatest allies in the battle for your family.

Supper Time

Someone asked me recently if I've always liked to cook.

I guess I have, I can't remember not liking it.

My sister-in-law Karen, told me she hated cooking but when she got married she knew she would have to do it so she decided to like it.

So she did, and today she's one of the best cooks I know.

I watch people cook, that's where I've learned the most.

Whenever I'm at someone's house and they're cooking, I'm watching, watching and learning.

I learned how to make pie crust by watching my sister-in-law Susan. I also learned how to chop an onion from her.

She never said here let me show you, I just watched while she worked.

I noticed the way her pie crust held together and took note of how it should look, then when I made mine, I knew when I had it right.

My Grandma Money is a wonderful cook. She always made cooking look easy. I learned to fry chicken and make potato salad from my Grandma.

Mark's mom is a cook without compare. She taught me to always measure accurately for consistent results.

Bake a cake at 325 degrees instead of 350 and it will be moister.

I learned to ice a cake and decorate a cake from Sandy Wright Porter.

I learned to can and freeze from my mother.

If you've learned to find your way around the kitchen, invite someone over and let them watch.

If you don't know a lot about cooking start looking and listening.

Being able to put a meal on the table speaks to the heart on a daily basis.

Decide to like the blessing of feeding your family. Look forward to the good things you can make for them.

Plan ahead and be prepared so you don't feel so frazzled about it.

Buy a fresh bouquet of flowers for the kitchen as you work and then when suppers ready put them on the table.

This is the kind of simple daily gift you can give your family and have them still be talking about it twenty years from now... They'll talk about how they felt when you called, "Supper Time" or where everyone sat and all those other things you recall from your own childhood.

So, while you're working on supper think of how thankful you are to have a family and how thankful you are to have the means to feed them and while you're being thankful, you might just drop a note of appreciation to that special person who taught you a thing or two about cooking.

You'll both be glad you did.

CPSIA information can be obtained
at www.ICGtesting.com
Printed in the USA
LVOW13s2253171216
517784LV00011B/936/P